THREADS

THREADS

UNRAVELING THE
MYSTERIES OF ADULT LIFE

BARRY WEINHOLD AND GAIL ANDRESEN

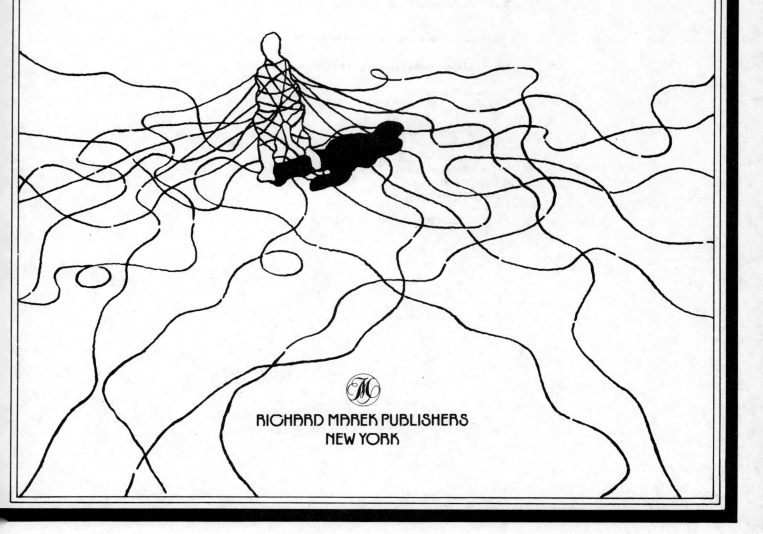

RICHARD MAREK PUBLISHERS
NEW YORK

Jacket and Book Design by Lynn Hollyn and Iris Bass

Library of Congress Cataloging in Publication Data

Weinhold, Barry K
  Threads.

  Bibliography
  1. Adulthood.   2. Personality change.   I. Andresen,
Gail, joint author,   II. Title.
BF724.5.W44   158'.1   78-31870
ISBN 0-399-90045-4
ISBN 0-399-90049-7 Pbk.

PRINTED IN THE UNITED STATES OF AMERICA

I greet the highest in you.
(Old Navajo saying)

This book is dedicated to those of you
who are willing to greet the highest in
yourselves and others.

CONTENTS

SECTION TWO
TECHNIQUES FOR CHANGE
AND GROWTH

SECTION III
APPLICATION OF PERMISSION THEORY
TO SPECIFIC ROLE GROUPS

ACKNOWLEDGMENTS

We are indebted to many people who have influenced and assisted us. We wish to thank our friend and teacher, Jan Vanderburgh, who reviewed the first draft of this manuscript and gave us the support and Permissions we needed to continue the project. We wish to acknowledge the contributions of Jan Johnson and Nancy Wood for their style editing of the manuscript, Fran Weinhold for her typing of the manuscript, and Joyce Engelson, our editor, for her patience and support.

We wish to acknowledge some of the threads we drew from other sources. The roots of Permission Theory were derived from script analysis, a part of Transactional Analysis Theory developed by Eric Berne. Other followers of Berne whose writings and works have influenced our thinking were Claude Steiner, who wrote *Scripts People Live*, and Robert and Mary Goulding. The Gouldings were the first to propose a list of common cultural script decisions. They postulated that in the process of growing up most people make similar decisions about themselves, other people, and the world they live in. Our list of eleven common script decisions was adapted from their list.[1]

Rational-Emotive Therapy, developed by Albert Ellis, also provided us with a useful way to understand the irrational ideas that people may use to restrict their lives. We are indebted to all of these people and all the others who have developed concepts that formed the threads for this theory.[2]

Others who assisted us at various stages of the production of this manuscript were Helen Andresen, Barbara Remmel, and Ruth Wild. We wish to acknowledge the presence of the countless threads from the lives of our students and clients without whose trust we could not have developed this theory or written this book. Finally, we wish to thank our families, who provided the continuous love and support we needed to write this book.

Barry K. Weinhold   Gail L. Andresen
Colorado Springs, Colorado Lakewood, Colorado

PREFACE

Many people are unable to break out of restrictive patterns. They want more happiness, satisfaction, and peace in their lives. This book is for anyone who is perpetuating self-defeating habits of living or is stuck in a pattern of reexperiencing unfulfilling situations. It tells how people get themselves stuck and the ways in which they restrict their options. It provides information and skills for unraveling these life tangles.

No matter how confused or inadequate you may have felt, no matter how messed up your life may have been, you can begin again. You can learn to cope with change and to be happier and more successful. What we offer you in this book is our unique and simple approach to solving the mysteries of adult life.

SECTION ONE

PERMISSION THEORY: THE CLUES FOR SOLVING LIFE'S MYSTERIES

1 PERMISSIONS: A BASIC TOOL FOR CHANGE

LIFE ONLY DEMANDS FROM
YOU THE STRENGTH YOU
POSSESS; ONLY ONE FEAT IS
POSSIBLE—NOT TO HAVE
RUN AWAY.

MARKINGS—
DAG HAMMARSKJÖLD

Permissions are positive messages from yourself, other people, and your environment that enable you to become happier, freer, and more successful. Permissions are everywhere and they are free. They are one of the basic tools for change. A Permission is:

—Reminding yourself to relax when you are feeling tense.

—Taking time for yourself at the end of a busy day.

—Asking for a hug from a friend or spouse when you want to be close.

—Having a friend say, "I like you just the way you are."

—Having a friend call you when you are feeling lonely.

—Reading a psychology book and finding out you aren't crazy.

—Being caught up in the rhythm and harmony of the "noises" of a subway in the morning on the way to work.

You can give yourself Permission, get Permission from others, and find Permission in your environment to enjoy any of these rewards of living. What is necessary is a decision on your part to take the first step.

Some suggestions that may make the first step easier are:

1. Consider yourself your own therapist. You are an expert on you. Although you may wish to seek professional help, you are still in charge of what you learn from and what you will do with the knowledge gained through therapy. This book is not a substitute for therapy, but your use of Permissions, along with the other information and skills contained in this book, may have powerful therapeutic effects.

2. Look at learning about yourself as a *process* and not merely a *goal*. The process of learning how to learn, unlearn, and relearn can be as exciting as learning why you do something. This book emphasizes process learning, or learning the process of how to be more effective or how to change your life if you don't like it. You may know that you are unhappy as an adult because you were abused as a child, and yet you remain unhappy. You still have to learn the skills and information about how to change your life before you can be more happy. This knowledge is essential.

3. Seek support from others. Changes are frequently difficult to make and maintain. It is therefore strongly recommended that you share your insights and changes with those persons willing to support those changes. You may wish to form a study group, using the activities in this book and a discussion of their personal application as a source of support. Your changes will affect others and their support is often necessary to maintain your new patterns.

However you decide to use this book, there are numerous techniques and activities here for you to use in your daily life. Practice in using these tools can help you increase your options and assist you in identifying and unraveling the threads that connect you to self-defeating patterns of living.

SEARCHING FOR CLUES

By now, you may be asking yourself, "Now that I have decided to take the first step, what do I do next?" A good place to begin is to look at the ways you stop yourself from getting what you want. The questions listed below may help you start your search.

WHAT ARE THE MYSTERIES OF YOUR LIFE?

Have you ever:
—Degraded yourself in front of other people?
—Had trouble letting go and having fun?
—Been afraid to show your real feelings?
—Found yourself repeating unsuccessful ways of doing things?
—Abused drugs or alcohol?

—Been depressed and not known why?

—Felt you had to play roles with other people?

—Been afraid to try something new and different?

—Been afraid to be close to others?

—Had an unsuccessful marriage or relationship?

—Found yourself doing the same things you didn't like your parents to do?

In the process of growing up, we all made decisions about 1. who we are, 2. who all those other people are, and 3. what the world is like. These decisions are some of the threads that attach you to old, maybe childish, ways in which you still think about yourself, other people, or the world you now live in. If you identify with any of the above situations, you may have decided that others are hateful, cold, deceitful, weak, rejecting; that you are dumb, unlovable, worthless; or that the world is scary, hostile, or crazy. If you use these decisions to control and direct your life, you may have created a narrow and limited existence for yourself.

Do you know how many distinct, separate thoughts you have during an average day? Studies have shown that most people have over 50,000 separate thoughts every day, and more than seventy percent of those are repeated every day.[1] They may be important or trivial thoughts, but they all influence your functions. The quality of your functioning is related to the quality of your thoughts.

You may repeat many of these thoughts until they are out of your awareness, but their effects are always present and visible for you or others to see. Your thoughts literally create your actions. *You are what you think.*

Where did all your thoughts come from originally? As far as we know, when you were born you didn't have any thoughts, only reflexes. Most of your important thoughts came directly from your parents and other adults who influenced your thinking as you were growing up. Some thoughts originate from the culture at large: the media, literature, and the social customs and mores you grew up accepting.

In tracing the threads from your past that are still influencing your life in negative or limiting ways, you will need to look at how the present patterns of your everyday thoughts fit together. To help you trace these threads, Permission Theory organizes these thought patterns into eleven common childhood script decisions. According to the theory, most children organize their thoughts into decisions about themselves, others, and the world around them. If these thoughts are not changed as one grows, these decisions remain in effect and help form the patterns of current thinking.

The following inventory may help you begin to identify those specific thoughts that are tied to various childhood decisions you made about yourself. It is important that you be honest with yourself in answering these questions. Honest answers could save you considerable time and trouble as you begin the exciting process of unraveling the major mysteries of your life and taking complete charge of your life.

DECISION IDENTIFICATION INVENTORY

Directions: Place a check in the column that best indicates what is true for you.

Decision Indicators	Degrees of Investment in the Decision Indicator			
	Hardly Ever	Sometimes	Usually	Almost Always
1. I don't believe I'm very worthwhile or important as a person.				
2. I wish I were a person of the opposite sex.				
3. I have trouble really "letting go" and having fun.				
4. I have a hard time putting my needs and wants first.				
5. When faced with a problem to solve, I get confused and don't know what to do.				
6. I don't seem to be able to know when I'm feeling sad, mad, scared or glad.				

Decision Indicators	Degrees of Investment in the Decision Indicator			
	Hardly Ever	Sometimes	Usually	Almost Always
7. I don't seem to be able to get close to people when I want to.				
8. I find it hard to deal with life's responsibilities.				
9. I have trouble finishing projects.				
10. Things I say and do seem "crazy" to others.				
11. I have difficulty trying new things.				
Column Scores				

Total Score

Scoring Procedure

Each item is scored as follows: Hardly Ever - 1, Sometimes - 2, Usually - 3, and Almost Always - 4. Go over each item and write the corresponding number in the column where you placed a check mark. Add all the numbers to get your column and total scores. Place your total score on the continuum below and look at the suggested interpretation of scores.

```
      11 _____
   22 _____ 44
```

Interpretation of Scores

11–16 Absence of major restrictive decisions.

17–22 Some early decisions are affecting your life.

23–28 Many early decisions are affecting your life.

29–34 You are not enjoying life very much.

35+| You have severely restricted your life.

While you were growing up, you may have acquired these thoughts from what your parents said to you or by observing them talking to each other or to other people. You, like many other children, may have learned many of your thoughts just by watching your parents or other important adults. Generally, the culture around you supported these thoughts and your parents probably helped you to interpret the world around you in ways that supported their beliefs, attitudes, and values.

You may have had to figure out the meaning of some of your parents' messages. For example, if you often heard "Don't bother me, can't you see I'm busy," you may have decided that you were in the way and your parents would be better off if you didn't exist. You therefore heard the message as "Don't exist," or "Grow up fast." These and other messages may have led you to the decision *I Won't Exist* or *I Won't Be a Child*. Many times these decisions are made from a position of "I'll show you." Once a decision is made, it is used as a way to organize your perceptions. You tend to perceive only those things which support the decision and not see those things that would not support the decision. These decisions help shape your world view. For example, persons operating on *I Won't Exist* decisions may devalue themselves and their contributions. They may avoid full involvement with others or see others as not valuing them or their ideas. They likely will not take good care of themselves: They drive too fast, smoke or drink too much, or become workaholics trying to prove their worth or importance.

The following chart shows the eleven most common childhood script decisions with some of the related *Do* and *Don't* messages people use to make these decisions.

COMMON CHILDHOOD SCRIPT DECISIONS[2]

Decision	Do and Don't Messages
I Won't Exist.	Don't live life to the fullest; don't be important; avoid rather than be active; don't exist (die).
I Won't Be the Sex I Am.	Don't be the sex you are; be tough like a man (for girls); be pretty like a girl (for boys).

Decision	Do and Don't Messages
I Won't Be a Child.	Grow up; don't act so silly; don't get taken care of—be independent; don't make noises; don't be physical or active; don't have fun; you have to struggle and suffer to get ahead.
I Won't Have Needs of My Own.	Take care of others; don't do what you want to do; don't ask for what you need; don't be important; don't be real; be what others want you to be.
I Won't Think.	Don't think or solve problems for yourself; act stupid; act confused; don't think about certain subjects; be symbiotic and passive.
I Won't Feel.	Don't have an awareness of your feelings (feel something else); don't express your feelings.
I Won't Be Close.	Don't be vulnerable; don't express closeness; don't experience closeness; don't accept closeness; don't risk letting others know you. (Be cool.)
I Won't Grow Up.	Don't do things that are adult; don't be independent; don't grow up and leave—be our baby; don't be sexual; don't be assertive.
I Won't Succeed.	Don't finish what you have started;

Decision	Do and Don't Messages
	don't set realistic goals; don't be competent; don't be effective; don't think of yourself as a success.
I Won't Be Sane.	Don't take care of yourself; scare yourself and others with what you say, do, or feel; let others take care of you.
I Won't.	Don't act; don't explore, be careful; the world is a scary place; don't be inquisitive (don't ask questions); block and inhibit yourself.

Your job is to identify these childhood decisions, connect these threads to your present patterns of behavior, and then learn how to change these self-defeating decisions and the patterns that are connected to them.

You may wish to go back over the Decision Identification Inventory you filled out earlier in this chapter. Each of those items is keyed to one of the eleven decision areas. See if you can match them up and notice which ones are present most frequently in your everyday thoughts.

Tracing the threads from your past is an important and exciting adventure to help you better understand the role of these decisions in your life today.

You, like so many others, may have decided that you have to accept what life hands you or make the best of your situation. Einstein wept when he thought about how little of his potential he actually used. Most of us, unwittingly, settle for so much less than what we could become or do. To quote R. D. Laing:

> What we think is less than what we know; what we know is less than what we love; what we love is so much less than what there is, and to this precise extent, we are much less than what we are.[3]

The saddest part of this dilemma is that one of the blessings we all enjoy in this country is considerable freedom to change our lives if we don't like them. Sure, we can't change everything we would like to, but we sometimes forget that our culture, unlike the many where tradition rules with an iron fist, offers us greater opportunities to change our lives. The simple fact is that most of us have not learned how to make use of this freedom. We still operate as if we are imprisoned by habit and tradition, even when we know that many of our values and beliefs are not serving our best interests. In other words, we are only as free as we decide to be. The following is an example of this concept:

Twenty-seven-year-old Anne, when she began therapy with us, was unemployed and unsuccessful in school, and generally did not like herself or her life. Anne had just returned from an abortive attempt to escape herself by hitching a ride to California and working in a massage-parlor flesh factory. She dressed as if she had just rolled a skid-row drunk and stolen his clothing. Nothing matched or seemed to matter. Her hair was long but without much life or shine; it hung limply over one shoulder. Her whole manner spelled failure and defeat. She appeared to be in a daze when we asked her, "What do you hope to gain as a result of doing therapy with us?" She answered in a quiet, down-trodden voice, "I want to feel better about myself; I don't like myself very much. Do you think you can help me?" We honestly regarded her as a poor risk for therapy based on her presentation, but we decided to take her on.

We worked with Anne for about nine months in an outpatient group and individual therapy. She worked hard during that time. Very slowly the results of that effort began to appear. She found a job she liked and became a respected leader among her co-workers. Recently, she wrote the following self-description, which validates most of the changes she made during this time:

"I am a gentle woman and have lived for twenty-eight years. My favorite things are learning and being with people. I now work with others who teach me much about myself. The importance of my life now is to share daily living with others who are still learning to think, talk, love, and be successful. I also have goals for my near and distant future. Daily, I accomplish these goals by attending to my pres-

ent needs. I fill each day with accepting success and sharing it with others. There is nothing about my past that you will miss by knowing me today. Tomorrow I will continue to create success and joy and love with those I meet."

Working with Anne was very rewarding and yet puzzling. At first we somehow missed how determined she was to change. Her statement about herself represents a foundation, the beginnings of a new life plan or script for her to follow. Obviously, she still has periods of time when the old patterns reappear. But the differences are found in her description:

"Now, if things seem to be collapsing around me, I know I will be able to handle them and I don't get bummed out."

Many people lead narrow lives and have realized, that they had the experience but missed the meaning. If you take a look at your life and don't like what you see, heed the words of Nadine Stair, age eighty-five.

If I Had My Life to Live Over

I would dare to make more mistakes next time. I'd relax. I would limber up. I would be sillier than I have been this trip. I would take fewer things seriously. I would take more chances. I would take more trips. I would climb mountains. I would eat less beans and more ice cream. I would perhaps have more active troubles, but I would have fewer meager ones.

You see, I'm one of those people who live sensibly and sanely year after year, day after day. Oh, I've had my moments, and if I had it to do over again, I'd have more of them. Just moments, one after another, instead of living so many years ahead of each day. I've been one of those persons who never goes anywhere without a thermometer, a hot-water bottle, a raincoat, and a parachute. If I had it to do over, I would travel much lighter.

If I had my life to live over, I would start barefoot earlier in the spring, and stay that way later in the fall. I would go to more dances. I would ride more merry-go-rounds. [4]

WHAT IS PERMISSION THERAPY?

Stated simply, Permission Therapy can help you understand the aspects of your life that may appear mysterious or confusing. It will help you trace the threads from your childhood experiences that can serve as clues to solving these mysteries. Using this theory, you can begin to understand how these threads from your past in the form of childhood script decisions may be still influencing your life. Finally, after you have understood these mysteries, the theory will show you how to change the decisions that no longer fit. Change is a normal part of life, and whether we like it or not, it is often necessary for us to learn more effective ways to manage change in our lives. Chapter II will provide an overview of the techniques you can use to change your life decisions.

GROWTH AND DISCOVERY ACTIVITIES

Answer each question in the space provided, or on a separate sheet of paper. We will give you an example on each one, but this is not to suggest in any way the kind of answers you should give. If you honestly don't remember, take a guess or leave it blank and go on to the next one. This exercise will help you put your finger on some clues to your threads extending into the past.

I. *Verbal Clues*

A. List ten words or phrases that best describe you. Example: kind, stubborn, lazy, intelligent, etc.
   1. _____
   2. _____
   3. _____
   4. _____
   5. _____
   6. _____
   7. _____
   8. _____
   9. _____
   10. _____

B. Go back over your list and put an M (Mother) or F (Father) by the words that your parents used to describe you as you were growing up. Example: If your mother used to say to you, "Sam, you are the laziest kid on the block!" put an M next to lazy. These words are clues to your threads of the past. You can think about how these labels still influence your life.

II. *Mixed Metaphors*

A. Various metaphors may provide clues to your childhood script decisions. Think about the common metaphors used by your parents when you were growing up. List them below. Example: "I'm at sea about that." "You have to get your feet on the ground."

_____

_____

_____

_____

_____

_____

B. Think about what kinds of script decisions might be connected to using these metaphors. List some thoughts and ideas. Example: "Don't think." "Be strong."

_____

_____

_____

_____

_____

C. Now, think about the metaphors you use today. Where did you first hear them? What meaning do they have for your script today? Example: "He tries, but he's all thumbs" is something you heard from Mother, and means "Try hard and don't make it."

_____

_____

_____

_____

_____

II TECHNIQUES FOR SOLVING LIFE'S MYSTERIES

YOUR REAL PURPOSE IS TO
IDENTIFY THE CORE OF
YOUR LIFE, THE CONSTANT
THREAD, THE CONSTANCY
IN YOU THAT PERSISTS
THROUGH ALL THE
CHANGING WORLD
AROUND YOU.
*WHAT COLOR IS YOUR
PARACHUTE—*
RICHARD NELSON BOLLES

This book contains six new self-help techniques—three basic and three advanced—that you can learn to apply to your life. These techniques are explained briefly in this chapter and developed more fully in Section Two.

BASIC TECHNIQUE #1: LEARNING TO FORGIVE YOUR PARENTS

The first technique is essential if you are to grow up and take charge of yourself and your life. You must learn to forgive your parents or nothing else will follow. Perhaps you are like the person who lived half of his/her life before discovering it was a do-it-yourself project! It may be hard for you to let go of old hurts and resentments you have held on to for years. Even if you have a lot to forgive, *you must do this for yourself.* It could be the most important decision you have ever made for yourself.

Hanging on to the old threads from the past may only serve to limit your happiness and effectiveness. Letting go of old hurts and resentments toward your parents is an essential step toward wholeness, as witnessed in the following clinical example of a client who was treated by one of the authors:

Judith was a friendly twenty-six-year-old, single female who suffered from periods of depression. When she got herself depressed she would sleep, frequently for days on end, completely withdrawn from the world. She had difficulty holding a job and keeping commitments.

I had been working with Judith on her periods of depression for about two months, meeting with her for one hour per week. During this time she often tested me to see if she could trust me and if I would support her if she really began changing. She missed appointments, showed up late, or at times acted confused in order to see what I would do. The last session really went well and I began to think she must have decided to trust me. We had talked repeatedly about her angry feelings toward her mother, so when she brought up this subject again, I seized the opportunity and asked her if she thought she was ready to forgive her mother.

Somewhat hesitantly she said, "I think so."

I asked her to go home and write out the following Permission message: "I now forgive my mother for all her mistakes from which I suffered." She was instructed to write that message several times on the left side of the page and write out any resistant thoughts or feelings on the right side of the page.

I wasn't sure how successful she would be, but I thought if nothing else the exercise would provide more clues about the sources of her resistances. The following week, when she arrived for her session, she greeted me at the door with a somewhat lighter than usual "Hi, how are you?"

Later, when we were ready to start the session, I asked, "Well, how did you do writing your Permission-to-forgive assignment?"

"I had trouble at first. I kept putting it off and finally worked on it last night."

"Tell me what happened when you wrote the forgiveness statement."

"I began to see what I was hanging on to and why I didn't want to forgive her. I was angry at her for not letting me get mad, and now when people do things that make me mad, I don't express it and I'm still blaming my mother for my depressed times."

"It sounds as if you are still hoping that by your getting depressed your mother and other people will feel guilty or responsible enough to finally give you the love and support you felt you never got."

"It seems silly to still hold out for that, but I guess it was easier to blame others than to learn how to express my feelings."

"You said 'was easier.' Does that mean you have decided to forgive her?"

"Yes, I really think so. Last night while I was writing out the forgiveness and my resistances, I finally realized that she really did what she thought was best for me and I have used her mistakes as excuses for not growing up and learning to take care of myself. Now I am ready and I feel strong. Perhaps the strongest I have ever felt."

"Well, that's a fine place to begin. What do you want to tackle first?"

BASIC TECHNIQUE #2: ASKING FOR PERMISSIONS FROM OTHERS

Another important skill is learning to identify the Permissions you need from others and subsequently using those Permissions to get what you are needing and wanting. You may know certain people who seem to be saying to you, "Yes, you can do it." You may not even be asking outright for their support. But they are a part of the support system you have arranged for yourself to make the changes you want. This technique emphasizes learning how to accept the support of others. Below is an example from my work with Judith:

Judith indicated that she was now ready to learn appropriate ways to express her feelings, particularly anger. I knew this would be a big step for her and spoke with her about joining one of my therapy groups. I reasoned with her that she was going to need a sort of laboratory where she could try out getting Permissions and support for her new behaviors. She needed a safe place to find out what would happen to her when she expressed feelings appropriately. I knew the others in the group, plus the group structure, would be more helpful to her than I could be in individual therapy. The group consisted of six other people, including myself. There were two men both in their forties and hoping to learn how to relax and enjoy life more. The other three women were all in therapy as the result of unsuccessful relationships. Two were divorced and in their midthirties, while the third was single and had just passed into the "over thirty" category.

During the first several group sessions, Judith again tested the safety of the group. She missed a session without calling to cancel. This was clearly an attempt to discover if these people cared enough to notice her and confront her on not following group rules (calling to cancel when you cannot attend). The following week the group responded to her in a confrontive but caring manner. I simply said, "I missed you, Judith." She seemed surprised when no one wanted to hear her reasons (or excuses) for not being there. They simply expressed how they felt about what she had done and asked her to recommit herself to following the ground rules.

During another group session I had an excellent opportunity to give her an important Permission. She was relating an incident where a co-worker had taken full credit for a project that she had worked on. I said, "Do you know you can express your angry feelings without losing other people's love and respect?" Judith looked at me for what seemed like a half minute and then said, "Yes, I know that in my head and I am also feeling that in my guts. I will let Sandy know that I was angry about not being recognized for my part in the project and ask her to correct the oversight."

BASIC TECHNIQUE #3: GIVING YOURSELF PERMISSIONS

This technique involves identifying the Permissions you need and want and then giving them to yourself. You may recall situations where you wanted to do something but held yourself back. You may have been temporarily immobilized by some fear and then you suddenly said to yourself, "Do it, go ahead and see what happens." This is an example of a Self-Permission, which is a skill you may use to help you support the changes you want to make. The example below shows how Judith used Self-Permissions:

Judith continued to seek Permissions from others in the group and occasionally reported asking for Permissions or getting Permissions spontaneously from other important people outside of the therapy group. At the same time she was learning to give herself the Permissions she needed.

One night during group, she opened up an important area for Self-Permission. She said, "I still have difficulty believing that my needs and wants are as important as those of others, particularly those of men."

I asked her to describe how she allowed that to happen with the men in the group. She related several instances in which she had given more "weight" to what the men had said than to what the other women and even she herself had said. I asked her to think about some Self-Permissions she could use to strengthen her belief in the importance of her own needs and wants. After several minutes of thinking silently, she said, "I'm going to start working with myself using the Self-Permission, 'I deserve love and respect just for being me.' I think the reason I listen to others more than myself is to get them to love and respect me."

I was glad that Judith came up with her own Self-Permission. It indicated to me she was beginning to internalize the use of Permissions. She may get stuck from time to time, but she now has some tools she can use to unravel her own threads and can return to that process when she needs to.

ADVANCED TECHNIQUE #1: USING PERMISSIONS TO HELP REWRITE YOUR SCRIPT

After building a foundation of new Permission information and an awareness of early childhood decisions, you can begin to rewrite parts of your script that no longer serve you. For example, if you decided as a child not to get close to others, you will need to change that decision. You will need to have new Permission messages that support your new decision: Getting close to others is normal and healthy and not dangerous to me. This process of script rewriting is illustrated below with Judith's work on this issue:

One of Judith's most difficult script changes involved giving up the illusion of control. Judith thought she could control others by being depressed or that other people could control her behavior. She worked diligently to overcome this attitude, following the forgiveness of her mother.

One evening during a group session, Judith was feeling low and seemed withdrawn from the group. After talking to her for several minutes I sensed that what she was saying was coming from her control illusion. I asked her if she was willing to try an experiment which might help her see through this illusion. She was willing, so I asked her to stand in the center of the group. I then said, "For the next fifteen minutes you are going to be a robot. You cannot do anything for yourself and can do only what the group members command you. We will not have you do anything harmful to yourself or others, but you will be under our control. You may now breathe normally and keep breathing at your normal rate."

Another member said, "Sit down," just as another shouted, "Take three steps backward." In the next few minutes everyone in the group was shouting commands to Judith. "Hold your left arm out in front of you." "Turn around." "Jump up and down." "Get mad." "Feel sad." "Be happy." "Stop thinking."

At first Judith tried to follow all commands, but soon found this was impossible. Finally, she yelled, "Stop! I can't do this anymore." I asked the group to stop and asked her what she had learned from the experiment. After sitting down and gaining some composure, she said, "I don't like being controlled and I realized that I chose to try to follow everyone's commands. In my life, I think I chose to let certain situations or people control me, and I know I can choose to accept the responsibility for my behavior and feelings. I can even choose to get depressed if I want to."

Intuitively, I knew that she was now ready to rewrite that part of her script. I said, "Judith, I would like you to experience that as a new script statement. Start by going to each member of the group and saying to him or her the following: 'I, Judith, have let go of the illusion that what others say and do has power over me without my full agreement.' Then say, 'I alone control my life and destiny.'"

She did this willingly and from each person she received Permissions and support for her newfound power. Finally she sat down, glowing with the realization of the power in her new position.

ADVANCED TECHNIQUE #2: USING PERMISSIONS TO MAKE REDECISIONS

As you update the parts of your script that no longer fit, you will need to learn to redecide the corresponding childhood script decisions and begin living your new decisions. Try putting your new decisions into action by actively expressing your feelings, your wants, your needs, etc.

This step was rather easy for Judith because of the work she did in giving up her control illusion. In fact, she made the new decision without consultation from me or from the group. She announced it to the group this way: "I want all of you to know that I have been using the Permissions I received last week and have redecided about taking charge of my life. I have given up pretending that anyone can hurt me without my Permission. I now know that I am in charge of my thoughts, feelings, and body and behavior. I have been living this new decision this week and I feel great."

I was very pleased with Judith's breakthrough, and I told her so, as tears of joy trickled down my cheeks. I asked her what she needed or wanted from me and the other group members. She replied quickly, "Nothing specific right now, and I will ask you for specific kinds of support if I need them. I would like to continue attending the group as a graduate for a while as I test my wings."

ADVANCED TECHNIQUE #3: USING PERMISSIONS TO STAY CURRENT WITH YOURSELF

When you have reached this stage, you will need to learn how to maintain your new decisions and your current knowledge of yourself. You will need to develop skills for keeping in touch with yourself: your needs, wants, thoughts, goals, problems, etc. If you accept change as a normal part of your life, then you will need to develop ways by which you can continually update your decisions and choices. Below are examples of some of the ways Judith learned to stay current with herself.

Judith continued attending group for several months and then her attendance gradually tapered off. My last contact with her started with a phone call. She said, "Will you let me take you out to lunch so I can tell you about all the wonderful things that are happening to me?" I accepted immediately and as I was entering the restaurant I was met by an enthusiastic "Hi" and a big hug. Judith was eager to share some of her joy. "You know, I have really learned to like myself, and what a difference that has made in all aspects of my life! My job is boring sometimes but I just don't let that get to me. Things that I used to let get me down for days, I now usually think my way through within an hour."

I was curious so I asked, "What things have you been doing to keep up with yourself?"

"Well," she said slowly, "I've been keeping a journal and learning how to keep track of myself. For example, I have noticed I want to establish an intimate, more permanent relationship with a man, and I've been working out that process for several weeks now."

"How's that working?" I asked with a smile.

"Great. I think I'm in love. I've met a man I really enjoy being with, and we are beginning to get more serious about the relationship. I am aware of recycling some adolescent myths about being in love, but this time without all that anxiety and pain I remember going through when I was fifteen."

SOME COMMON CONCERNS AND QUESTIONS ABOUT PERMISSION THEORY

Concern #1: "Won't it take years of psychoanalysis or deep therapy to come up with my original script decisions, the ones you say I need to be aware of in order to change?"

Answer: No. Most people, after reading and learning about the basic eleven decisions, can identify, by their present behavior, the threads from at least one childhood decision and then begin to change. It takes only one to start. Oftentimes identifying these threads leads us to a tie with other decision areas. Psychoanalysis, or other therapies which emphasize long-term probing to uncover childhood influences, can be helpful but are not necessary for you to begin changing your life.

Concern #2: "Can I still use Permission Theory even though I don't remember much about my early childhood?"

Answer: Even though you may have difficulty remembering your early childhood, what is important is your present behavior. By looking at what you are doing, saying, or feeling now, you can begin to trace the threads back to some possible decisions you made as a child. Even if you can't remember specifics about your childhood, you can still utilize Permissions to change decisions that are no longer useful in your present life-style.

Concern #3: "How do I know if I am remembering things from my childhood as they really happened?"

Answer: You don't! However, what is important is your perception or experience of what happened and your feelings about early events rather than what really happened. Your perceptions of your childhood are what have influenced your behavior, not what actually happened.

Concern #4: "I gave myself Permission to stop smoking, yet I am unable to quit. What else can I do?"

Answer: Perhaps quitting smoking isn't what you really want to do yet. Your smoking could be related to a script decision, and you could be attempting to quit for the wrong reasons. Some people decide to quit in response to a message that they *should* quit rather than deciding to quit because they *want* to. Permissions work best when they are prescriptive. For example, you can decide that you are important and are capable of taking good care of yourself. However, continuing to smoke may indicate some threads still tied to a childhood decision that you are not important. Viewed this way, giving yourself Permission to stop smoking was not a failure; it may have been the incorrect thread. If that happens, you can usually find the right one for you.

Concern #5: "Can I expect Permissions to work the first time I try them?"

Answer: Yes, in some cases Permissions will work immediately. However, the amount of "investment" or the relative number of threads attached to the decision may determine how long you take to change a particular decision. Also, you may engage in some trial-and-error learning before you find the best Permissions for you. The more you practice using Permissions, the better you will get at selecting the correct ones for you to use.

Concern #6: "In the past I have not always known what was 'best for me.' Will Permission Theory tell me what is best for me?"

Answer: No. You are the only person who knows what is best for you. However, sometimes you may need to hear what others think is best for you. If you are operating from a destructive script decision, Permission Theory can assist you in recognizing how you limit yourself, and it can provide you with information and skills to make new decisions that are better for you.

Concern #7: "Isn't giving myself Permissions going to make me more selfish, self-serving, and hedonistic?"

Answer: No. We believe everyone wants to feel valuable, lovable, and capable, all necessary ingredients for happiness. Happy people who have a positive sense of self are in the best position to be genuinely unselfish in their treatment of others. Some people attempt to manipulate others by calling them selfish. You may have allowed these people to make you feel guilty for seeking ways to get your needs and wants met.

GROWTH AND DISCOVERY ACTIVITIES

The following activities may help you search for clues to your mysteries.

I. *Parental Patterns*

   A. Write down the main advice your father gave to you while you were growing up. ("Be a good boy.")

_____

_____

_____

B. Write down the main advice your mother gave to you while you were growing up. ("Work hard.")

_____

_____

_____

C. Make a list of the favorite expressions or slogans that your parents used when you were a child. ("People are judged by the company they keep.")

_____

_____

_____

_____

D. Go back to A and B and make a list of the ways you have followed or not followed your parents' advice. ("I tried hard to do what others wanted"; "I was always uncomfortable when I did something I thought my parents wouldn't approve of.")

_____

_____

_____

_____

_____

E. Go back to C and make a list of the ways these expressions and slogans have influenced you. ("I have had trouble trusting others outside my family.")

II. *Missing Pieces*

A. What do you wish your father had done differently in raising you? How do you think you would be different?

_____

_____

_____

_____

B. What do you wish your mother had done differently in raising you? How do you think you would be different?

_____

_____

_____

III. *Waving Your Magic Wand*

A. If by some magic you could have changed anything about your childhood, what would you have changed?

_____

_____

_____

B. If by magic you could change anything about yourself now, what would you change?

_____

_____

_____

III PERMISSION PATTERNS

OUR LIVES ARE SIMPLY
THREADS PULLING ALONG
THE LASTING THOUGHTS
WHICH TRAVEL THROUGH
TIME THAT WAY

MANY WINTERS—NANCY WOOD

There is a story of a man being held prisoner in a small cell. He spends his time standing at one end of this dark, narrow world on his tiptoes. His outstretched arms hold on to the bars of the only window high above him. If he holds on tight and strains his head upward, he can see a few rays of bright sunlight shining through the window. He sees this light as his only hope for survival and will not risk losing it. He has become so committed to not losing sight of that light that it never occurs to him to explore the rest of his cell. As a result, he never discovers that the door at the other end is not locked. Ironically, he has been free from the beginning to walk out into the brightness of the day, if only he would let go.

We all hold on to old ways of thinking and doing things and consequently we don't live our lives in the full brightness of the day. We settle for a few rays of light and thus severely limit our vision. By examining your threads you may learn about the ways you have restricted your life. Picture, if you will, your threads as strings attached to people, places, and situations from your past. Notice if these strings are limiting your mobility in any way. Perhaps what came to mind just now could be clues for you to use solving your own mysteries of adult life.

By the time you reached adolescence you may have already made many of your important life decisions about how to get along with yourself, others, and the world. These decisions became the foundation for your life plan which, if you do not change them, will remain steadfastly the same until you die.

The three main reasons these early decisions may have had negative influence on your life are:

1. You probably made these decisions when you had a limited amount of information about other options open to you. As a child, your major sources of information were your parents and other important adults, like your teachers or relatives. If you followed their verbal and nonverbal instructions about how to get along in the world, you may have made decisions about living in a world that no longer exists. Kahlil Gibran wrote, "Your children are not your children. . . . You may give them your love but not your thoughts. . . . You may house their bodies but not their souls. . . . For their souls dwell in the house of tomorrow, which you cannot visit, not even in your dreams."[1]

Unfortunately, your parents, like most, were probably unwilling or unable to let you grow up without strings attached to their cherished beliefs. Your job is to cut the strings you no longer want or need, not out of anger but out of gladness.

2. You no doubt made important decisions while you were under some form of duress. Many of our clients and friends report remembering exact situations where they finally made life-shaping decisions. Sarah remembered an incident which happened when she was ten years old. Her mother came home falling-down drunk, an event Sarah remembers as happening quite frequently at that time. Sarah remembers saying clearly to herself, "I will never get this close to anyone again. It hurts too much to love someone who just doesn't seem to care." This is an I Won't Be Close decision, one that has been difficult for Sarah to change so she could trust and love others again. As an adult she has spent considerable energy acting strong and pretending not to need others.

3. Finally, you probably made most of these decisions while you were still dependent emotionally, financially, and socially. This dependency certainly limited your options and may have created the belief that you had no other choices. Following a severe reprimand from his parents, seven-year-old Steve said the following, "I hate you and I'd run away from home, but I can't drive and I don't have any credit cards."

Although these decisions are made during your childhood, their devastating effects may not show up until twenty, thirty, or forty years later. They were the adaptations you made to get along in your family, and as such they set a pattern for your development well into adulthood. These decisions may be the threads that show up later in broken hearts and broken lives.

TEST YOURSELF

Your attitudes about change can make change easy or difficult for you. This inventory is designed to help you find out more about your attitudes toward change in your life and how they may be affecting the search to unravel your mysteries. No one is asking you to change your attitudes, but instead to acknowledge what they are. As you discover your attitudes, you may wish to alter some of them if they do not reflect your current feelings. These attitudes are thought patterns derived from your past decisions.

THE OPENNESS-TO-CHANGE INVENTORY[2]

Directions: Place a check mark in the column that best represents how you see yourself. Please answer every item.

	Never	Sometimes	Usually	Always
1. I am open-minded and optimistic toward new ideas.				
2. Making changes in my personal life seems to take too much energy.				
3. I allow my fear of the unknown to keep me from changing aspects of my personal life.				
4. I am willing to risk trying something new even if I may fail.				
5. I tend to get confused when I think about changing aspects of my life.				
6. When I think of changing aspects of my life, I consider my wants and needs				

	Never	Sometimes	Usually	Always
before those of others.				
7. I actively seek information I want or need to help me make changes.				
8. I have two or more people who generally support me in the changes I am making.				
9. I tend to persist or stick with changes that I have decided to make.				
10. I am aware of the major reasons I do what I do.				
11. When I make major changes in my life, I find my feelings get in the way.				
12. People can "talk me out of" changes I want to make.				
13. I believe I have considerable freedom to change major aspects of my life.				
14. I am really hard on myself when the changes I plan don't work out.				
15. I tend to blame other people when the changes I plan don't work out.				
16. I have accepted change as a part of my personal life.				

	Never	Sometimes	Usually	Always
17. I have found that things I plan to change hardly ever work out.				
18. When I decide to change something about my life, I make a contract with myself.				
19. The changes I have made in my personal life have come as a reaction to pressures or changes from other people.				
20. I don't seem to know what I want to change about myself.				
Column Scores	/			

Total Score

Scoring Procedure

Each item is given a weight of 1, 2, 3, or 4. Certain items are keyed with the "Always" column weighted at 4, and others are keyed with "Never" and weighted at 4. The key below shows how to score each item.

Items scored 1, 2, 3, 4 (Never = 1, Sometimes = 2, Usually = 3 and Always = 4): Numbers 1, 4, 6, 7, 8, 9, 10, 13, 16 and 18.

Items scored 4, 3, 2, 1 (Never = 4, Sometimes = 3, Usually = 2 and Always = 1): Numbers 2, 3, 5, 11, 12, 14, 15, 17, 19, and 20.

Go over each item and write the number in the column where you placed a check mark. Add all the numbers to get a personal score on openness to change. Place your score on the continuum below and look at the interpretations of your score.

20   50   80

20–29 Premature hardening of the categories.
30–39 Awareness of discontent—may not be willing to take action yet.
40–49 Ready to start some small changes.
50–59 Build a support base for change and proceed with change.
60–69 Openness to change is apparent.
70+ The sky's the limit.

As you continue to read this book, be aware of your attitudes about change and where these attitudes come from. Watch how you let these attitudes color your feelings about what you are reading.

PERMISSIONS FOR LIVING FREELY

As you read on, you will find information about the common areas in which people typically limit their adult lives through childhood decisions. If you find that you have limited your life similarly, you likely will find the tools necessary for you to change those decisions. You can be as free as you want to be. You can:

—Be an important and valuable person.
—Be the unique man or woman you want to be.
—Play and have fun without having to justify yourself.
—Put your needs and wants first and actively find satisfaction in them.
—Think through and solve the problems you face in your life.
—Be in touch with and find healthy expression for your basic feelings (mad, sad, glad, scared, etc.).
—Experience spontaneous intimacy and closeness with others.
—Take care of yourself and be a responsible person.
—Explore your world safely and creatively.

Permissions exist everywhere, but you may not have been aware of them. Your decisions often determine what you see and what you do not see. As you read this book, you will probably identify the Permissions you still need and want.

PERMISSION CHECKLIST

Look at each of the following Permission messages and place a check mark beside those you believe would be helpful for you to remember and use in your everyday life.

_____ You are important.
_____ You can take your time.
_____ You can relax.
_____ You can make mistakes.
_____ You can play and have fun.
_____ You are fine just the way you are.
_____ You can be successful.
_____ You can ask for what you want and need.
_____ You can come first.
_____ You can be spontaneous and creative.
_____ You can take care of yourself.
_____ You can enjoy what you are doing.
_____ You can change yourself if you want to.
_____ You can _____ . (Fill in your own.)

The process of discovering Permissions can happen anywhere, as described in the following example.

June, a forty-five-year-old woman, was sorrowfully recounting to a close friend how she had spent much of her life doing things for others. Her belief was that only after she helped satisfy the needs of others could she think about satisfying her own needs. The friend looked into June's eyes and said, "You can come first; you are important and so are your needs."

June looked at her friend and frowned in disbelief. Slowly the message began to sink in and a joyous smile replaced the frown. June said, "Yes, I am important, and I feel good about being important to myself."

You, like June, may be listening to script messages that say your needs and questions are not important. For instance, have you ever felt self-conscious about asking questions in a seminar or class, because you felt others would think you were ignorant? If this is so, and you want to change the way you are living your life, you will need to develop a new set of messages. These are your Permission messages. When the old messages are hindering you, you need to begin searching for new messages that help you get what you want.

You will probably begin your search by being attracted to new sources of Permission. You may find yourself talking to people who you believe are living their lives the way you want to live yours. You may impulsively begin to read books, listen to music, or go to movies as you search for the Permissions you are needing. You may decide to begin therapy, join a club or a discussion group, or you go places where you believe you will find those new messages. At first you may not know what you are searching for, and then as you begin to find new Permissions, you will know how to make use of them. (Of course, some of you already have traveled far down the road of self-discovery and know what Permissions you need to hear right now!) You may, for example, need to know that you really are a lovable person.

Usually after some exposure to Permissions from one source, you will find the same messages from other sources, and then after hearing them from a variety of sources, you can begin to generate your own. Eventually, you will learn to use the new messages to replace your old script messages. Here's a beautiful example of learning to accept a new message:

Mason was a tall, handsome man in his thirties. He had potent messages not to express his feelings, especially sadness, and most certainly tears. He believed crying was, for men, a sign of weakness, endangering his tough image of himself. However, after Mason went through a traumatic divorce, leaving two beautiful children with his ex-wife, he began having strong feelings of grief and a great need to cry. One night he visited a female friend who was not threatened by tears. She said, "Did you know it is healthy for you to cry about missing your children?" Mason looked rather astonished and said, "I haven't cried since I was a kid." She responded, "You can cry any time you want, and you can start now."

Mason took a deep breath and asked, "Will you still like me if I cry?" She answered, "Of course I'll still like you. In fact, I'll feel even closer to you." Rather sheepishly, he asked in a small voice, "Will you hold me? I feel rather silly and very sad." She put her arms around him, and he began to let the tears out until they flowed quite naturally. She gave him much nurturing and encouragement.

After that incident, Mason began to allow himself to cry when he felt sad and lonely. He cried at sad movies and at other times. Sometimes he still hears the old message saying to him, "Be strong and don't cry." But he remembers his friend's encouraging words and now believes crying is healthy and good for him, not a sign of weakness.

Ask yourself:
—When was the last time I cried?
—What was the situation?
—How did I feel about crying then?
—What messages do I have about crying?
—Do I want to change my messages about crying?

GROWTH AND DISCOVERY ACTIVITIES

After reading this chapter, take time to do some or all of the following activities.

I. *Messages and Permissions*

A. Using your non-dominant hand (to get the feeling of being a child), write as many negative messages as you can remember getting from parents, teachers, or other adults while growing up. These are the messages you wish you hadn't received, and in looking back, you believe they had some harmful effects. Write them as *Don't* messages ("Don't be so serious") or *Be* messages ("Be more like your sister").

_____

_____

_____

_____

_____

B. Now list the ways these early messages still affect you. For example, a message that you had to be perfect may manifest itself in your thinking, "I still am very critical of myself and won't try anything new unless I am sure I'll be good at it."

Message	Effects

C. Make a list of the messages you wish you had received while you were growing up. (Again, use your non-dominant hand.) For example, "You're neat." "You think clearly." "I love you."

D. The messages under C represent some of the Permissions that you might still be wanting or needing. These are clues to the decisions you may have made because you were denied certain Permissions while you were growing up. You can learn to give them to yourself or get them from people you trust. The next several chapters will provide more information on this process.

II. *What I Need, What I Want*

A. Make a list as long as you can, starting each item with "I need _____." Example: "I need approval from others."

_____

_____

_____

_____

_____

_____

_____

B. Now, go back and rewrite the same items, but this time change the "I need _____" to "I want _____." Examine each item to determine if it is really a "want" or a "need" item. If you can't survive without it, then it is a legitimate need. All others are really wants and do not have survival issues attached to them.

_____

_____

_____

_____

_____
_____
_____

III. *What I'm Scared to Do, What I'd Like to Do*

A. Make a list of six to eight things that you are really scared to do. Start each with "I'm scared to _____ ." Example: "I'm scared to learn to swim."

_____
_____
_____
_____
_____
_____

B. Go back, examine each item you listed in A, and ask yourself, "Whom am I pleasing by being too scared to do that?" List the messages you used in deciding to scare yourself about each item. Example: "I'm pleasing my mother and grandmother, who were scared of water. They said, 'If you have to go swimming, don't go into the deep water—you might drown.'"

_____
_____

_____
_____
_____
_____
_____

C. Go back and examine the items you listed in A and determine which ones you would like to do but haven't done because you have been too scared. Then, list them in the left-hand column. On the right side of the page list the Permission messages you would need, to do what you have wanted to do.

Example:
"Learn to Swim."

Example: "You can learn to swim safely and decide how to take care of yourself in the water."

To Do List	Permission Message
_____	_____
_____	_____
_____	_____
_____	_____
_____	_____
_____	_____

IV FOR EVERYTHING THERE IS A TIME

THE FARTHER BACKWARD
YOU CAN LOOK, THE
FARTHER FORWARD YOU
ARE LIKELY TO SEE.
*MY EARLY LIFE: A ROVING
COMMISSION*
—WINSTON CHURCHILL

All of us are, at any given moment, the sum total of everything we have ever experienced: the time we took our first step as a baby, the time we cried and no one picked us up, the time we had our first sexual stirrings, and the time we felt most alive.

Your development has consisted of a continuous arranging and rearranging of your experiences in order to solve new problems and learn new tasks encountered at each stage along the way. For instance, when you were a child you may have learned how to open and close a door, only to discover a door with a lock on it that wouldn't open. Thus, the next problem to solve was how to open a door with a lock on it. Each unsolved developmental problem and each unlearned task is threaded into the next stage of development, where a new set of problems and tasks awaits you. In addition to being continuous, development involves recycling anything not previously solved or learned.

Fred came into treatment because he feared losing his job, his wife, and his son. He looked concerned yet spoke flippantly the first time. He was short and stocky and had thick wavy black hair, which he carefully combed from a side part. Fred confessed that he was a stubborn man at his job. Often he was reluctant to do tasks others asked him to do. He seemed to dig in his heels several times every day, much to the irritation of his co-workers. He had lost several jobs for being uncooperative. One evening Fred told us that his mother was continually forcing him to do things he didn't want to do. He had experienced life as a power struggle for as long as he could remember. He even admitted he could see himself in the behavior of his two-year-old son, with whom he had a tremendous amount of conflict. He shared a recent incident when he and his son were playing on the floor with blocks: He and his son fought over who got the big flat block. He said his wife had to break it up—remarking that she didn't like living with *two* two-year-olds. Unsolved two-year-old and new twenty-two-year-old problems may be occurring simultaneously.

You might ask, "Why do I remember some of my childhood experiences and not others?" Freudians might explain that some early trauma may have caused you to repress certain events or circumstances. Perhaps after years of analysis, you would begin to understand how these previously repressed experiences are still affecting you today. By contrast, Permission Theory offers you the opportunity to discover how you became who you are today without lengthy and expensive analysis. According to Permission Theory, you remember certain experiences and forget others based upon the various script decisions you made. You usually can identify these decisions using the childhood experiences you do remember. After some initial identification of these decisions, other, forgotten experiences are more likely to be remembered. The rest of this chapter will provide you with actual case studies of persons who identified the eleven most common script-decision areas. You may identify many of the threads to your childhood messages as well as the specific childhood decisions you made as you read these case examples.

THE ELEVEN MOST COMMON SCRIPT DECISIONS

The following case histories were those of clients we worked with separately in therapy. The therapist in each case was one of the authors.

I Won't Exist

Diana recalled:

My mother named me after a close deceased friend of hers. Mother told me my birth was a difficult one; it was as if I somehow didn't want to be born. Her doctor finally induced labor and used forceps to pull me out.

I was terrified of my father. He would "punish" me with a silent, disapproving stare. His eyes burned right through my soul! I cannot escape that icy glare even now. He looked as though he hated me, rather than my actions.

When I was five years old, my parents got a divorce. My father moved to another state and I seldom saw him. At about this time, I began to have violent temper tantrums when I didn't get my way. I threw myself down the stairs once and gashed my forehead.

I often thought I was somehow responsible for my parents' unhappiness. Many times I thought everyone would be better off if I were dead.

Now, at twenty-six, I have decided to seek therapy to deal with these issues. Shortly after beginning therapy I began working on letting go of a lot of the anger I felt toward my parents. The other group members and Barry, my therapist, were supporting me in identifying what my feelings were. During several recent group sessions I had felt myself getting to very early experiences, including images and thoughts about my birth.

Even so, my rebirthing experience was certainly a surprise to me. It began while we were doing some breathing exercises at the beginning of the group therapy session. As a result, I began to identify feelings of sadness. I immediately got a sore throat as I apparently tried to disregard this new awareness. As my sadness continued to emerge, I clenched my fists and my jaw, afraid to let go of my feelings. Barry was supportive and gave me Permission to express my feelings, and at the same time, he helped me open my jaws. I sort of screamed-cried for a while as images of both parents flashed through my mind. This crying was frightening and I wasn't able to control it.

I was then directed to a mat and pillow. I was unable to lie flat on my stomach on the mat. Persistently, I chose a position with my knees folded up and my face buried in the pillow. Sobbing came easily but there were no tears. As I cried, I felt new space inside around my heart and lungs. I also could feel my energy flowing from my throat to intestines without any blocks.

I stopped crying to analyze my feelings and suddenly realized I was in the womb. There was a blackness darker than I'd ever experienced. By now, I was curled up in a fetal position on my side. I could not deny any longer what was happening to me. I said to Barry, "I'm not born yet!" I was more surprised than scared now, and support from the group was critical. I knew I did not want to stop. My only awareness centered around the sound of Barry's voice. He was talking to me about being born, and the sound of his voice was very important and helpful.

I actually remembered not wanting to be born! This seemed almost humorous. How could I not want to be born? I was already twenty-six years old. I had my eyes closed and I remember seeing the image of a large hand about to hit me. My fear of being born turned out to be another important step, and I really needed to be reassured in order to accept it. I was amazed to be able to make the actual decision to be born. It had never occurred to me that I had any choice. Barry told me that I indeed could choose whether or not I wanted to be born. When I had worked through my feelings of surprise and fear, I was just asked to decide. I was still afraid and I asked Barry, "Are you going to slap me?" It is clear now that my image of a large hand hitting me was that first slap. When Barry answered "No," I had a deep sense of relief and made the decision.

Once again I was crying like crazy but I still had no tears. My cry was more of a yell, and I don't remember hearing this kind of sound before. It was a very fearful, helpless, uncontrolled scream. My body began to pull up involuntarily, and I had no control over my body. After a final yell, I panted and panted until I was completely out of breath.

To check out whether or not I had completed my "rebirth" process, Barry asked, "How do you know you are alive?" My answer to this was beautiful and simple.

"I am breathing and it really feels good." I was exhaling from spaces I'd never felt before.

Suddenly I felt cold and "curled up." Barry wrapped me in a blanket and held me, and I felt content and secure. It seemed as if I was being taken care of for the first time in my life. I then experienced all my senses except taste. I was distracted by colors and textures, and I could feel Barry's voice emitting very calm, comforting feelings as he talked to me. Wow! That is the way to communicate with babies. The whole thing was a truly joyful experience!

I Won't Be the Sex I Am

Judy walked into my office with long, confident strides. Her hair was cropped short and she wore a Fifth Avenue doubleknit suit with vest and tie. Her auburn hair, freshly shampooed and shining in the light, framed a serious yet good-looking face.

She began, "I was named Judy after Judy Garland, and my mother was disappointed that I didn't turn out all fluffy and feminine. When I was very young, my father and mother got a divorce. Naturally, I was very upset because I was a 'daddy's girl' and I knew I would miss him.

"Dad said to me, 'Judy, now that I am not living with you anymore, you will have to be the man in the family and take care of Mommy. I know that you will do a good job and that I can rely on you as if you were my son.'

"I was scared about having to be the man in the family, and I decided the only way I could do it was to pretend I was like a man. I didn't play with dolls or other girls' things. As I grew up, my father said he wanted me to be a physicist, and I was so afraid of rejection from him that I went to college specifically to fulfill that challenge. I remember wishing many times that I was a man because I thought it would please my father more.

"I am forty years old and I did become a physicist, but I'm missing something in my life. Because I still strongly wish I were a man, I am reluctant and scared to establish permanent relationships with either men or women. I am lonely. . . . If only I'd been born a man!"

I Won't Be a Child

Merrill was having sexual problems with his wife. He wore his hair pulled straight back and slicked down with oil, which made him look older than his age, forty. He was thirty pounds overweight, and his clothes were drab and unbecoming.

He recalled, "They said that when I was born, my mother couldn't stand my crying. She also couldn't stand it when I was loud or acted like a kid. Later I remember her saying, 'That's my little man,' or 'Big boys don't cry,' or 'Shut up and act your age!' When she was particularly upset, she would yell, have tantrums, and do all the things she hated me for. . . . Yes, I felt she hated me. I grew up fast to survive.

"When I was in school, I was not liked much by other kids, mainly because I didn't play with them. I felt they were too juvenile and silly. My teachers would have me help them because I was so mature. The kids called me 'teacher's pet' and made fun of me.

"I remember I was scared of girls and didn't date until I was in my late twenties. I met my wife and married her without our really knowing each other. She says she wishes I weren't so serious and would 'let my hair down' and have fun. I enjoy watching football on TV, but mostly, I guess, I am pretty dull.

"My wife doesn't feel very sexually turned on by me. She says that I'm not exciting, and she wants sex with me less and less. I'm worried now that she may take a lover or divorce me. I don't know what to do."

I Won't Have Needs of My Own

Ginny sat in a chair in a crumpled heap. Her eyes were glazed over, and she was unresponsive and very depressed. Her hair was uncombed and she hadn't bathed in several days.

In a small voice she hesitantly remarked, "I was one of fourteen children, and I didn't know my father very well. I only remember him coming home drunk and stumbling up the stairs to bed. There was rarely enough to eat and my father spent a lot of money on booze. One winter, my mother tore up an old chair to use for firewood to keep us warm. I never asked for anything because asking seemed futile. I owned three dresses and one pair of shoes. We shopped at Goodwill for necessities. I learned early that my needs would not get met, so I decided I wouldn't have needs.

"In school I was unpopular and sick a lot, and received poor grades. I didn't think very much of myself.

"I got married at age fourteen and started having babies because that was all I knew to do. Now I'm forty-eight and going through a divorce. All I want to do is die. Without my husband, I'm not able to cope, nor am I really worth anything. I gave him everything I had; I took care of him, anticipated his every wish, cooked for him, and now he is leaving me. I don't want anything from anyone. I just want to die."

I Won't Think

Sam recalled that during most of his life others pointed out how poorly he thought and solved problems. He said, "Once, playing catch with my father, I was hit in the face with a ball because I looked away when a friend yelled, 'Hey, Sam.' I was only five or six at the time. My dad and others laughed at me and said, 'Poor Sam, didn't think to catch the ball before looking away.'

"Even as a little kid I was a real daydreamer. My teachers and parents got on my case about it. They would say, 'He's off in his own world again. That boy—he's always daydreaming.'

"When other kids were making models or using Erector sets, I occupied my time collecting baseball cards. My mom often told me that I got too wrapped up in those goofy cards.

"In junior high school, I ran around with what my dad called 'the wrong crowd.' Actually they were a bunch of nonachievers who did 'cool' things; they smoked cigarettes and drank booze.

"My parents and teachers told me all the time how lazy and stupid I was. I think the climax came in my senior year in high school when the counselor told me to go to trade school because college would be too much for me. I was really angry and had thoughts like, 'I'll show them I can go to college.'

"I fantasized that when I graduated from college I would shove my degree in that counselor's face. For the first time, I really wanted to make something of myself.

"Now, sometimes, I sit back and evaluate my life. I have tenure as a teacher, I make about twelve grand a year, have a three-bedroom house, a wife, and daughter. I've done all right, but I sometimes feel that I've done a lifetime's work and have already hit my peak. I get scared of what's ahead.

"My goals in life have changed a bit. I don't want to be complacent; I want to continue to improve myself. I am going to use my own intuition and see what happens. I am a big boy now, and I can use my resources to leave some type of 'mark.' Pride in what I am and can do has changed me. Pride is the biggest reward I can get for changing. I now know I can think, and I will think and solve my problems effectively."

I Won't Feel

Jan is thirty-two years old, a mother of two, and just beginning to unravel the mystery around her depression. She traced the threads to an *I Won't Feel* decision during childhood and adolescence. She recalled the beginnings: "My mother has told me that when I was small I did not want to be held or cuddled. She said I pulled away when she tried to hold me. My father told me that, as a baby, I smiled almost continuously. My aunts told me I smiled when anyone looked at me. Thus, I must have learned early to cover up my true feelings with a smile.

Jan related the following experiences she recalled about elementary school. "In first grade, I was very unassertive. I remember buying an ice-cream cone, and when walking back to school, a little boy in my class walked by and took it. I continued to walk, barely glanced back, and did not protest at all. My sister, Marge, who was three years older than I, was mean to me when we were children. I remember an incident that resulted in her slapping me across the face. I did not retaliate or express any feelings; I didn't even cry. She stood there looking at me and laughed because I did not defend myself. I felt very hopeless."

As a teenager, Jan continued to reinforce those hopeless feelings. She said, "When I became extremely anxious or angry, my vision would sometimes become distorted. Objects would shrink and reappear at a great distance. As a teenager, I went through a period when I cried about everything. I didn't know why I was crying and my teachers just ignored me. My family became either very irritated or angry with me. My sister teased me about being a crybaby.

"I made the decision not to feel when I was fifteen, after I wrote a poem about my despair and hopelessness. My mother found the poem and read it. She became very frightened and angry and refused to believe I had written the poem. I felt very angry and isolated, so I decided to hide all feelings from her and never again let her know how I felt.

"I have been very angry with my husband at times, but rather than allow myself to express it, I become depressed. I withdraw and take my revenge out in sneaky ways. I feel good that I now recognize my anger and allow myself to feel it. I still have difficulty expressing anger well, but I do allow myself to feel it. Also, I now usually realize when I am setting up someone to blame so that I can express my anger."

I Won't Be Close

Rob recalled that he began to withdraw from girls when he was very young. He said, "I remember that I was three and a half when I first saw my little sister fresh from the hospital. I didn't like her because she was a girl. I remember I didn't enjoy playing with girls as I grew up, and I didn't like being hugged by female relatives. I only felt comfortable being hugged by my mother.

"Even then I was more interested in things than in people. I remember once playing with a cousin until he became angry at me and stomped on my toy race car. He told my mom that I got mad at him and broke it. The only thing I remember feeling was sad about the race car because it hadn't done anything to get broken up.

"In high school, I didn't go to school parties, dances, or parties at someone's house because girls were there. I wanted people to know that I wouldn't go places where girls were present. I went to one dance in high school, mostly due to my parents' insistence, and I felt so 'out of it' I never went to another one.

"I had very few dates between eighteen and twenty-four. By then I didn't mind being with girls as long as I wasn't seen with them. I didn't like to be questioned about any girl I dated. I finally did care about one girl, who very suddenly started going steady with another fellow. I was hurt and angry with myself for even getting interested in a girl.

"Between twenty-four and twenty-eight, I wanted to date but was afraid to ask girls out. I was afraid they would refuse and afraid they would accept. I was always scared of conversations because my communication skills were terrible. At twenty-eight, I thought a change of location would change my life so I turned over a new leaf and headed west. Living here where no one knew me, I began to break my old patterns. Now, at thirty-five, I am happily married, and much of my past seems almost as if it happened to someone else."

I Won't Grow Up

Georgia described herself as a thirty-six-year-old single woman who had tremendous anxiety and a deep inferiority complex. She said, "I hate my lack of self-discipline and my inability to make decisions. I have a hard time coping with everyday problems, and I am painfully shy around most people.

"My mother always considered me to be mature beyond my years (I can't understand why) and to be very independent (how little she knew about me). I know she always hoped I would marry so she could be a grandmother.

"I can't imagine not feeling anxious. I may seem poised at times, but my insides are usually like Jell-O. I'm always worrying about what could happen.

"I wish my mother had been a mother

to me. If she had disciplined, helped, talked with, and supported me, I think I would not be so insecure, defensive, and hostile.

"I wish my father had allowed me to know him and had taken the time to get to know me. If he had verbalized his love for me instead of substituting for it with material possessions, I would have felt more secure. Because of our ambivalent relationship, I can't seem to have a realistic relationship with a man. I am afraid I cannot have a prolonged satisfactory relationship with any man. If my own father couldn't love me, no man can or will.

"If I could magically change anything about myself, I think I would like to be about five years old and begin my life again. I would change everything about myself. I would be a very confident and responsible person, eager to participate in every phase of life—good or bad. However, I am not really convinced I can change thirty-six years of miserable self-conditioning."

I Won't Succeed

"I was an only child, and I remember I constantly disappointed my parents because I couldn't do all the things they wanted me to do." Charles, a forty-one-year-old chemist, is unraveling the dynamics of his *I Won't Succeed* decision.

"I became fat from overeating when I was eight or nine. I liked to spend much of my time alone fantasizing about things I would do someday. These fantasies were generally of a grandiose, heroic nature or a 'someday I'll show them' variety. I stayed alone with toys, and I felt nervous around other kids. I felt my parents forced me into competitive activities with others. I was constantly challenged to prove myself, and the 'real' me was never good enough. Because I was often lonely and suspicious of others, I decided to act, on the outside at least, as if I didn't need anyone. I felt very bitter and hostile toward most other kids; I hated them.

"I was a sprinter on the high school track team, and I often 'set myself up' to lose. I became very nervous before a race, and as a way of dealing with the anxiety, I would think of excuses for losing. I would tell myself that I couldn't run as well in the morning, or that I couldn't run when it was too cold. I even thought that the guy who won wasn't really better but had somehow psyched me out. I always said to myself, 'I could have won if I'd really tried,' but somehow I never felt very good about it anyway.

"I really admired my dad, but he often made me mad. I wanted to be better than he was. I remember I ran away from home at fourteen because he had told me he had run away from home when he was fifteen.

"After I got married and finished school, I always felt my dad was pressuring me to succeed. He was always worried about money. For Christmas he would give us huge amounts of money as gifts and I always felt bad because I couldn't match his gifts. He worked hard and invested wisely, and when he was forty, he sold his business and retired.

"I remember as I approached forty, I began to spend long hours trying to figure out how to make enough money to retire by forty. I had some wild schemes involving land, oil, or investments, but none of them worked. I ignored my family and my regular job as a chemist during most of this time; consequently my marriage and my job went sour. When I reached forty and hadn't made it like my dad, I felt like a complete failure. I left my wife and family because I thought they were to blame for holding me back. I tried to have fun and forget about all that, but I had trouble sleeping and was jealous of the woman I was seeing.

"I still haven't worked all this out, but I am beginning to change my standards for success. I am having more fun and doing what I want. I think I have turned a corner in my life, for now there is so much to learn that I never get bored."

I Won't Be Sane

Margaret talked freely about the threads connected to her *I Won't Be Sane* decision. "When I was eight or nine, I was afraid I would go crazy. I remember listening at the door as my parents fought. My father vowed to kill a neighbor man and my mother. It was the beginning of a nightmare which was never really over. I think I must have felt I was somehow responsible.

"For years there was a dark, gloomy cloud over the family. I never knew what horrible situation I might find at home. I was hurt and disgusted because my father began to drink heavily, and I was terrified when he began to carry guns.

"When my mother didn't like something I did or said, she would say, 'You're just like your father.' When I was nineteen the family went on a vacation and my father got severely depressed. I remember thinking how much I was like him.

"Once when I was in junior high school, I talked back to my mother and told her I was really scared of something (I don't even remember what). She said, 'God will punish you for having thoughts like that.'

"If we watched TV and someone expressed strong feelings, she told me to turn off the TV. She said, 'I don't want to hear that stuff.'

"I had a lot of fears and doubts about myself when I was in high school. I remember thinking, 'If I tell anyone how I feel, they will think I'm crazy.' My father went 'crazy' again shortly after I was married at twenty-three. He got really angry and smashed everything he could get his hands on. His own father had died in a mental institution, and a doctor said Dad had premature senility.

"Things built up inside me until I thought I couldn't cope with anything or anyone. If my kids made even the smallest demand, I yelled and screamed and cried and sometimes even hit them. Afterwards, I felt terrible and hopeless. I'm not in control of my life."

I Won't

Although Alice's mother bought her a variety of clothes, Alice wore the same dress every day, month after month. She washed and ironed it about every three or four days. "I just don't know myself unless I wear that dress, and I won't wear something else."

Alice, who made an early *I Won't* decision, is thirty-three and lives with her parents. She is almost totally dependent, has no job or income. She resents doing chores around the house and enjoys watching television or reading books.

"I'm very quiet and not at all sociable. I say 'Yes' when I mean 'No,' and then fail to follow through with my commitments. I think I'm a hopeless case. My mother says she didn't hold me to feed me; rather, she propped up my bottle on a pillow. She was too nervous to hold me and only touched me when I needed a diaper changed.

"When I was small, my mother would sit me in a corner and forbid my exploring around. She said there wasn't sufficient space to crawl in our one-room apartment. I was overweight as a baby and am overweight now as an adult. I've tried, but I guess I won't lose weight because I'm not very sociable anyway.

"I was a good student in school, I liked to read, and I earned excellent grades. I had visions of becoming a historian or a lawyer or a famous writer. I still would like to write, but I know I won't because I don't have any drive.

"I don't like being this old and still living at home with my parents, but I know I won't change or do anything about it."

AUTONOMY OR SLAVERY

All of the eleven decisions described in this chapter represent attempts to make others responsible for various aspects of your life. If you identified with any of the above decisions and you don't change them and reclaim the lost ground you gave away to others, you may lead a narrow, limited, and dependent life as an adult. You will not solve your personal mysteries of adult life and may never learn how to break out of the self-imposed slavery you created for yourself.

You may, like most people, strive for autonomy, but you can't achieve it if you remain unaware of the threads that tie you to childhood decisions and inaccurate information about yourself, other people, and the world. You can continue to blame your parents, society, or others for not preparing you properly for an autonomous life. If you didn't prepare yourself for autonomy while you were growing up, you now have to begin learning how to be autonomous as an adult.

Because they believe they should be autonomous as adults, many people *pretend to be autonomous*. People begin weaving themselves masks or facades to hide behind in order to prevent others from seeing their true fears and vulnerability. You may be angry, scared, or sad about your plight, but nothing will produce real autonomy short of learning how. One of your greatest fears may be If my parents or other people aren't to blame, then I must be to blame for it. What is missing in the syllogism is that blame has very little to do with what is real. It is an invention, a pattern of thoughts and behaviors you wove together to help you avoid autonomy. The fact is, you created your own experiences; so they belong to you and no one else. The obvious alternative is open to you: If you don't like what you have created, then create something else more to your liking.

According to Permission Theory, *everyone has a natural drive toward autonomy*. Because of our present cultural beliefs, values, and child-rearing practices, few people reach adulthood with enough psychological maturity to live happy lives. This book will help you prepare to achieve higher levels of psychological maturity, and to realize your authentic self.

GROWTH AND DISCOVERY ACTIVITIES

Introducing Yourself to Your Parent and Child. Picture in your mind one of your parents or a significant parent figure (aunt, grandparent, etc.). Go back in your memory to a time when you were a child. Picture what your parent looked like then, what your parent said and did, and everything you can remember about your parent. When you have recalled these things, proceed with the exercises below.

A. List at least three things this parent said and/ or did that you really liked. Example: "You sure are pretty"; "You will be a success someday."

_____

_____

B. List three ways a child would feel being around a parent like this. Example: happy, good, etc.

_____   _____   _____

C. List at least three things this parent said and/ or did that you did not like. Example: "You are driving me crazy"; "You are a bad kid!"

_____

_____

_____

D. List three ways a child would feel being around a parent like this. Example: mad, intimidated, etc.

_____   _____   _____

E. Use three adjectives to describe what you remember most about this parent. Example: harried, mean, gentle, etc.

_____   _____   _____

F. List three ways a child would feel being around a parent like this. Example: agitated, fearful, etc.

_____   _____   _____

G. Recall a situation in your childhood when you misbehaved or broke a rule. Describe the situation in terms of what you said and did. What did this person do? How did she/he treat you? Example: "I remember when I was five, I stole some of my father's cigarettes and lied to him about it. He found a bent one in my pocket, took it out, and spanked me with a hair brush. He said, 'I'll teach you to never steal from me and lie about it again!'"

_____

_____

_____

_____

_____

H. What did you feel, and what did you do as a result? Example: "I felt guilty and angry. From then on I decided to go 'underground' so I'd never get caught again."

_____

_____

I. List at least three messages (verbal or nonverbal) that this parent gave to you or about you. Example: "She's as clumsy as her father."

_____

_____

_____

J. What decisions about yourself, other people, and the world do you think you made in response to these messages? Example: acting clumsy.

_____

_____

K. Now, look back over your answers. Do any of the things you wrote about your parent figure in A, C, E, G, and I apply to you today? Example: "Yes, I am still not open in my actions with others. I suppose I'm still operating 'underground.'"

_____

_____

_____

_____

_____

L. In what ways are you like this person? Example: "I'm like my mother in that I'm bossy to my children and I cry easily." (List at least three.)

_____

_____

_____

M. In what ways are you not like this person? Example: "I'm tidy and take pride in my appearance." (List at least three.)

_____

_____

_____

N. In what situations do you find yourself currently feeling or acting as you described a child would feel or act in response to your parent figure? Example: "Oftentimes I feel guilty if I don't do something I'm supposed to."

_____

_____

_____

_____

O. In what ways do you find yourself treating your children the way _you_ were treated when you misbehaved as a child? Example: spanking them or yelling irrationally, etc.

_____

_____

_____

P. Which messages sent to you as a child are you still listening to? Example: "You are clumsy."

_____

_____

_____

Q. How do you think these messages are affecting you today? Example: "I won't try anything new, because I fear failing."

_____

_____

_____

R. Ask yourself: "Do I want to continue listening to these messages?" Go back to Q and check the messages you wish to change, and remember these for later reference.

V   TRACING THE TIES TO YOUR PAST

THE SECOND HALF OF A
MAN'S LIFE IS MADE UP OF
NOTHING BUT THE HABITS
HE HAS ACQUIRED DURING
THE FIRST HALF.
THE BROTHERS KARAMAZOV
—FEODOR DOSTOYEVSKY

THE HAND THAT ROCKS THE CRADLE RULES THE WORLD

A newborn baby receives many nonverbal messages from parents, who reinforce them again and again during childhood. When you were a baby, you learned about the world through your mother's and father's responses to your needs and wants. You learned, intuitively, in the process of being fed, held, touched, and stroked, what kind of person you were *expected* to be.

Alma was a new, nervous mother, who was resentful of having to give up a career as a geologist to stay at home with her new baby daughter.
The baby was unplanned and created many changes in life plans. Alma handled the baby roughly, yelled at her when she cried, and in general was very rejecting of the newborn.
The baby was learning she was unwanted and unlovable.

THE PRIMARY SYMBIOSIS

The primary symbiosis between mother and baby is normal and healthy and is most clearly defined during the nursing process. When a baby cries, a mother who is breast-feeding experiences a releasing sensation in her breasts, and this feeling triggers her inner need to nurse her baby. The baby's hunger is satisfied, and the mother's breast tension and fullness are relieved. Primary symbiosis is usually resolved at the age of two or three. The resolution of the symbiosis occurs when par-

ents set appropriate limits allowing their children to solve problems and actively develop effective ways to take care of themselves. Overprotective or underprotective parents may make the resolution of symbiosis difficult. Problems arise when symbiosis is maintained beyond this age.[1]

Many people carry unresolved symbiosis issues with them into adulthood. Smithy was a teenager who had no responsibilities around the house. In fact, his mother laid out his clothing and cleaned his room for him. Smithy was essentially being treated like an overprotected two-year-old. Despite his mother's opposition, Smithy later married a woman who continued his mother's caretaking. Interestingly, his mother was unable to attend Smithy's wedding because she had a mental breakdown.

Smithy's mother needed to take care of her son to prove her worth, and Smithy had learned to rely heavily upon her. The two could not function effectively without the symbiotic attachment established in Smithy's childhood. Smithy had found a substitute, but his mother had not.

In the following developmental chart, we have outlined the normal stages of development and tasks you would normally go through. This chart is a ready reference to identify stages and to assist you in identifying tasks which you may not have completed. Later we will discuss how you can recycle missed or incomplete developmental stages. The focus now is to weave together and finish as many of the incomplete tasks as possible, so that the result is a happier you.

NORMAL DEVELOPMENTAL CHART[2]

Developmental Stage/Age	Tasks to Be Completed
Early Oral (0–6 months)	Developing attachment and symbiosis Seeking stimulation through active sensory means

Developmental Stage/Age	Tasks to Be Completed	Developmental Stage/Age	Tasks to Be Completed
	(putting objects into your mouth) Deciding to live Learning the difference between self and others		like Mommy or Daddy.")
Oral Exploratory (6–18 months)	Active exploring of the environment Testing separateness Autonomy in self-feeding and locomotion Cause-and-effect thinking ("If I cry, someone usually comes to pick me up.")	Latent (6–12 years)	Concrete thinking Learning reasons for rules Learning to argue, negotiate, or debate other points of view Developing own parent-testing values and beliefs Activity orientation; learning to do things to get recognition ("strokes") ("If I do a good job on my report, my teacher will praise me.")
Anal (18 months– 3 years)	Deciding to think and solve problems Giving up illusion of control ("I can't control my parents with my temper tantrums anymore.") Learning to make social contracts; respecting rights and feelings of others	Adolescence (12–18 years)	Developing physical autonomy Recycling any leftover problems Developing a value structure, rather than a rule structure ("This is what I believe.") Sexual experimentation
Genital (3–6 years)	Incorporating the culture Distinguishing fantasy from reality Learning to control impulses; reflective thinking ("If I wait until Mommy is off the phone, I can ask her to play with me.") Sex-role identification ("I like to play dress-up to look	Young Adult (18–25 years)	Emancipation from parents Establishing an independent stroking economy ("I get my important strokes from my close friends.") Establishing long-term relationships Economic autonomy Deciding to follow a life-style

Developmental Stage/Age	Tasks to Be Completed
Adulthood— Creation (25–40 years)	Learning to keep social commitments ("I will do it because I agreed to do it.") Being productive Recycling any unresolved childhood problems with one's own children
Adulthood— Reevaluation (40–60 years)	Reassessing life-style and script Trying out missed experiences ("I have wanted to travel and now I'm going to do it.") Recycling any unresolved problems
Adulthood— Resolution (60+ years)	Accepting the inevitability of death Recycling dependency issues and control issues ("I don't want to be a burden, but I can't stand being alone.")

THE TIES THAT BIND

Your early script decisions were woven tightly into your total being by parental and social pressures and woven at a time when you had little knowledge of alternatives.

A crying baby who is rarely picked up may decide, "It is not safe for me to have needs" (*I Won't Have Needs of My Own*). A baby who is held carelessly and who is occasionally dropped may decide, "This world is not a safe place for me" (*I Won't Exist*). A baby who gets a diaper pin stuck in his/her skin and is left to cry may decide, "Hav-

ing feelings gets me nowhere" (*I Won't Feel*). A mother may prop up a bottle with a pillow and ignore a child during feeding and thus foster a negative decision (*I Won't Exist*). What did you decide as a result of what happened to you when you were a baby?

A mother wanted a girl for a second child after having a male child first. She gave birth to another boy and almost totally rejected the child. She refused to feed and care for him in any way, so the neighbors had to intervene before the baby starved to death. Finally, the baby was taken away from his mother and placed for adoption (*Don't exist* and *Don't be the sex you are*).

A frequently absent father who refuses to pick up his baby, or to pay any attention to him, sends a definite message: *Don't exist.* A mother who force-feeds a child before he/she cries for a bottle provides a *Don't have needs of your own* message.

As a child, you eventually decided which messages you would listen to, and the threads of your script developed from these decisions. How you reacted to messages received during childhood determines how you see yourself, other people, and the world around you.

Linda was five years old when she expressed anger with her mother for not letting her go to a friend's birthday party. She said, "I hate you! You are mean and ugly."

Her mother smacked her in the face and said, "Don't you talk back to me again, or I will send you away to live with the gypsies."

Linda decided she had better not feel or express anger again. Instead, every time she felt angry, she got scared and used this scare to block her anger. As an adult, Linda has a low awareness of angry feelings until they build up, and then she attempts to justify them by blaming others or situations for things that happen to her.

As an adult, when you experience situations that remind you of an original script decision you made, you may reexperience aspects of the situation with intense feelings. You may feel that you are in great danger, or that you might even die. In reality, the situation may be uncomfortable, but usually you are in little danger at all. These exaggerated feelings are valuable clues that can help you recognize "here-and-now" situations that are tied to early decisions. Thus, when you are experiencing a situation in which your feelings are more intense than the situation calls for, you probably are remembering a thread that is tied to the survival or safety feelings experienced in the original situation.

Jack married Mary, a small woman who was about the same size as his mother. Mary, like Jack's mother, took care of him. Jack often acted stupidly about doing things around the house. Mary Rescued* him by saying, "Here, let me do that!"

Jack would then respond angrily, "Bug off and leave me alone; you're always interfering." Jack was really responding to his own angry feelings with his mother, who had Rescued him as a child. Jack subconsciously "set up" the Rescue so that he could blast out angrily at his wife (mother). Jack was recycling unresolved anger over and over instead of solving the archaic dependency issue with his mother.

Awareness of the old issues and the way they continue to influence you is the first step that induces you to change. You can acquire awareness by thinking back over your life to key times, highly emotional experiences or times of crisis, by remembering stories told to you by your parents, grandparents, and other important people in your life. These awarenesses will lead you to understand the intensity of the survival and safety feelings and will help you to identify the discomfort-level feelings associated with the here and now. Understanding how to separate the archaic threads from the here-and-now elements in a situation is essential to changing.

Mario had a very unsuccessful student-teaching experience, mainly because he chose to work with a traditional sixth-grade teacher whose teaching philosophy was the opposite of his. In examining why he chose to work with her, he suddenly realized that she reminded him of his own sixth-grade teacher, who had severely criticized him. Apparently Mario had sub-

consciously created the situation to work out his unresolved feelings about his own earlier experience. He had been aware of the destructive elements in the situation and inadvertently set himself up to fail again. Armed with a new awareness of the situation, Mario resolved his feelings in therapy and went on to complete his student teaching successfully.

According to Permission Theory, people recreate current examples of earlier unresolved situations in order to get them resolved once and for all.

SCRIPT DIRECTORS AND PRODUCERS

Healthy parents, teachers, and other people can assist children to make healthy decisions while they are growing up. Therefore, healthy adults help produce healthy children.

During the school year, a class of seven-year-olds had acquired a used aquarium. Some of the children volunteered to each bring in a fish. After several weeks of carefully and lovingly tending their "fish family," one of their favorite fishes died. Kerry, who had recently lost her father in an automobile accident, burst into tears about the dead fish. Some of the other children felt uncomfortable about her expression of sadness. The teacher quickly sized up the situation and said, "It is fine for you to have sad feelings about our favorite fish." During this time, the students could evaluate their own sad feelings and could redecide that having sad feelings was acceptable. Not only was Kerry sad about the fish; she was recycling sadness about losing her father. The messages she heard from the teacher were reassuring and supportive to her growth as a healthy child.

Being healthy, emotionally and physically, is not synonymous with being perfect. The perfect parent, teacher, or other significant person, does not exist. Children need parents, teachers, and other role models who can react with real feelings and thoughts. These are caring people who are effective at solving their own feelings.

*The word Rescue is capitalized to distinguish it from legitimate rescues. A Rescue is doing something for other people that they can do for themselves. It is a common way people attempt to increase their own self-esteem, while reducing that of others.

LEARNING THE ROPES

Script decisions affect the whole being of an individual. Evidence of decisions can be found in everything you do or say or in the way you look and carry yourself. People you consider "pains in the ass" may be those people you are afraid of, and in their presence you literally tighten your sphincter muscles. They may remind you of people you were afraid of when you were young.

Watching people breathe, sit, or stand can give you clues to the threads of your own scripting. People with *I Won't Feel* decisions may breathe shallowly and may stoop their shoulders to protect themselves from experiencing their feelings. People with an *I Won't Think* decision often have deep frown lines in their forehead. *I Won't Be Close* is often seen in obese people or those with strong offensive body odors. For many overweight people, the basic *I Won't Feel* or *I Won't Be Close* decisions are often not activated until they are within five pounds of the weight they think they hope to get down to.

Barbara is a compulsive dieter who is always successful until she approaches her desired weight. Then she becomes scared and agitated, a state which usually continues until she does the only thing she knows will stop the scared feelings—she goes on an eating binge.

DRESS REHEARSALS

Certain principles and concepts are involved in the process of changing early script decisions. Some of the main ones are *Permissions, clout,* and *support.*[3] By learning how to use these concepts, you can take charge of the process of becoming who you want to be. *Permissions,* as we stated in the introduction, are everywhere. You can learn to find the specific Permissions you need. The exercises at the ends of the chapters in Section One can be used to facilitate your discovery process. Instead of listening to the old messages in your head, you can give *clout* to someone you trust and to whom you decide to listen. You may require *support* while you are in crucial phases of your change process, and may find it through friends, relatives, or your spouse.

GROWTH AND DISCOVERY ACTIVITIES

I. *Prenatal History Fantasy Trip*

Fantasize being inside your mother's uterus before you were born.

A. What do you imagine your mother said when she first found out she was pregnant with you? Example: "Hurrah, I'm pregnant!"

_____

_____

B. What do you imagine your father said when he first found out he was going to be a father? Example: "That's great!"

_____

_____

C. Check which level you think may have been appropriate for your birth situation.

wanted/planned	I'm lovable and capable and so are you.
wanted/unplanned	I'm lovable and capable and you are not.
unwanted/planned	I'm not lovable and capable and you are.
unwanted/unplanned	I'm not lovable and capable and neither are you.

D. Based on the above information, what do you imagine it was like for you inside the womb? For instance, what do you imagine your mother was like?

suffering	underweight	unhappy
overweight	unhurried	fearful
took care of self	weight OK	angry
relaxed	worried	happy
contented	smoked	healthy
sick		
other _____		

E. What do you imagine your mother's relationship was with your father while you were still unborn?

emotionally remote	angry	happy
physically removed	scared	healthy
tense	close	loving
other _____		

F. If you could have heard what was being said and discussed about you while you were still in the womb, what do you imagine the messages were? Example: "I hope it's a girl!"
1. Messages you imagine were given by your mother: _____

_____

Messages you wish your mother had given: _____

_____

2. Messages you imagine were given by your father: _____

_____

Messages you wish your father had given: _____

_____

3. Messages you imagine were given by close friends of the family or relatives (grandparents, aunts, uncles, nieces, nephews): _____

_____

Messages you wish others had given:

_____

II. *Fantasize Your Birth*

A. How would you describe your actual birth process, including your reception into the world? Example: hospital atmosphere, air conditioning, forceps, slap on rear, forced labor, irritable doctor.

_____

_____

B. What sorts of messages would you have heard as you entered the world? Who was there, and who would have said what? Example: "He looks just like a judge." (Doctor, nurses, mother, father)

_____

_____

C. What messages or things were said about you the first few days of your life? Who said what? Example: "He sucks like he means business." (Father) _____

_____

_____

D. What environment were you born into? Describe your family, living conditions, socioeconomic status, housing, etc.

_____

_____

_____

E. What birth order were you (first, second)? What effect, if any, did this have on you? Example: "As first-born, I had greater responsibility to be as my father wanted me to be." _____

_____

_____

III. *Script Birth Announcement Card*

A. Name
1. Who named you? _____
2. For whom were you named? What significance was there? _____

_____

3. If you had named yourself, what name would you have chosen?

_____

4. How do you think others reacted to hearing what your name was? (Did they think it "fit" you?) _____

_____

B. Weight, Length, and Physical Features
1. Like whom do you imagine they said you looked physically? _____
2. What do you think your father/mother wanted to hide about you physically? _____

_____

3. What do you think your father/mother wanted to show off about you physically? _____

C. Date and Time of Birth
1. What is the story that is told about the final events leading up to your

birth? Example: How your mother got to the hospital, etc. _____

_____

2. Did you arrive before expected, on time, or later than expected?

_____

3. What significance was attached to the date and time of your birth?

_____

D. Place of Birth
1. Describe the immediate surroundings of the place where you were born (hospital, home, taxi, etc.).

_____

2. Town or city _____ State _____ Country _____.
What significance was attached to your being born in the above places?

_____

E. The Proud Parents
1. Who was present at your birth? _____

_____

2. What significance do you imagine was attached to those present at your birth?

_____

3. What do you imagine your mother told others about you? _____

4. What do you imagine your father told others about you? _____

_____

F. Gifts
1. What gifts do you think your parents received for you? _____

_____

2. If you had sent a gift to yourself, what would it have been? _____

_____

G. Announcements
1. Did your parents send or give out birth announcements?
   Yes _____ No _____
2. If so, to whom do you imagine your parents sent or gave birth announcements? _____

_____

H. Write Your Own Birth Announcement: If you were reborn today and could write your own birth announcement, what would you write about yourself? (Use a separate page if necessary.)

_____

_____

_____

VI PARDON ME, YOUR SCRIPT IS SHOWING

MOST OF US BECOME
PARENTS LONG BEFORE WE
HAVE STOPPED BEING
CHILDREN.

PETER'S QUOTATIONS—MIGNON
McLAUGHLIN

NEW WAYS OF UNRAVELING YOUR LOOSE THREADS

Like many people, you may have grown up hauling a whole set of ghosts with you. You may still listen to messages you received from your parents as if they were standing behind you telling you what you should and should not do. To check yourself, write down all the things you can think of starting with "I have to _____." Then go back and start each item with "I choose to _____." instead of "I have to." Any items that you can't translate into "choose to" are probably ghost messages to which you are still listening. For example, Priscilla, an immaculate housekeeper, believes she has to have her house spotless and everything tidily in its place before she will allow anyone in for a visit. She admits she feels a heavy compulsion to cleanliness and recognizes she can't choose to be messy but rather feels she has to be tidy. She remembers her mother was also very tidy and as a child Priscilla got punished severely for not keeping her room immaculate. Priscilla is obeying her ghost messages to be clean as a hard-and-fast rule that she allows to run her life. Strange as it may seem, even breathing, living, or dying are *choose to*s.

The reason you, like many people, continue to give yourself and others these ghost messages is that you may still want your parents or others to be responsible or to blame for certain aspects of your life. You are still behaving like a powerless child in some areas because you probably felt powerless when you made your original script decisions. To check yourself in this area, write down all the things you can think of starting with "I can't _____." Then, after you have made an extensive list, go back and change the "I can't" to "I won't _____." Again, if you have any

items on your list that you *"can't"* change to "I won't," these are the ones which indicate that you most likely are listening to ghost messages of decisions gone by.

The process of making childhood script decisions is one of "making" someone else responsible (to blame) for your life itself (*I Won't Exist*). Any redecision you make (an action to change the original decision) has to be made from an autonomous position after you have given thoughtful consideration to the real alternatives available. You must also have a clear picture of how such a redecision will benefit you. You can make a decision to appraise your strengths and weaknesses realistically. One way to do this is to assess the amount of energy you wish to put into being successful. Another way is to maintain a clear idea of the enjoyment you will probably get from being successful. You may also think about whom you are still blaming by not being successful. ("If my dad had only insisted that I take Latin in high school, I could have gotten into medical school and become a doctor.")

Larry grew up hearing his mother say, "Larry, you can't do that." As a result of hearing this repeatedly, Larry grew up having problems with being successful. He had plenty of ideas about how to succeed, but he had difficulty following through on any of them. He was still listening to his mother's expectations that "he couldn't do it." In discussing his blocks with a counselor, he decided to stop listening to his mother's messages and to go ahead and give himself Permission to be successful.

PARENT PATTERNS

All people can grow up in a healthy environment, get accurate information, receive support and loving guidance, so that they can make healthy decisions about themselves. Until recently, much of psychology was interested in studying the unhealthy side of human development. Now the focus seems to be shifting to include the study of what people need so that they grow up healthy. From what we now know, it is clear that effective parenting is a very difficult task. It requires training that involves both skills and information. It also involves parents' learning how to get their own needs met in healthy ways.

> John's father tried to control him. His father ruled with a heavy hand, and John resented the control. As a parent himself, John wanted to raise his kids differently so they wouldn't resent him. However, when he saw his kids getting better parenting than he himself had received, he felt resentful. He was angry with his children, and, ultimately, he tried to control them the way his father did him.

THE GUILTY PARENT [1]

All parents in our society are guilty of not being successful parents. No parent has ever been completely successful in giving all the love, care, knowledge, or support that his/her children need and want. To some degree all parents are failures as parents, and yours are no exception.

This condition is caused mainly by the impossible demands we place on parents in our society. We say to parents, "You should know how to be successful naturally, without ever learning anything about parenting." When parents do learn how difficult parenting really is and how little they know about it, they often get really scared. They say to themselves, "I have to be a good parent and I should know how." When parents realize they can't meet society's or even their own internal standards for being "good parents," they experience a real double bind. What most parents do with this bind is to try to *appear to be successful* and to get very defensive if anyone questions their parenting skills. In order to maintain the appearances of success, your parents probably attempted to control you so that you would grow up to be successful, loving, and obedient. Then you could be living proof of their success as parents, and they could show you off to the world as a product of their good parenting.

To insure their "success," they remained tied to you and demanded that you "listen to them" instead of seeking other sources of parenting which they feared might lead you astray. They may have tried to make you feel guilty for wanting to be independent and for wanting to seek other parenting sources. In short, they found it difficult to let you grow up. Sensing your parents' vul-

nerability, you may have learned to manipulate them by "pushing their guilty button" to get what you needed or wanted (*I Won't Succeed* because "It's your fault that I don't do well in school").

Everybody needs supplemental sources of parenting to get additional nurturing. However, like most children, you probably believed you "should" get all that you needed from your parents. When you discovered you couldn't get enough, your responses may have included feeling cheated, getting angry, blaming your parents, and pushing harder on their guilty button. You may have even rebelled, run away, or done destructive things in a desperate attempt to make your parents give you what you wanted and needed. Most criminals are still trying to blame their parents or parent substitutes, such as teachers, policemen, judges, or even society for not giving them what they wanted and needed.

As long as you continue to blame your parents or others for not giving you all you needed and wanted, *you will never grow up.* Growing up requires that you forgive your parents for not giving you enough parenting and then actively seek the new sources of parenting you still need and want. You can't afford to wait for your parents or parent substitutes (spouses, teachers, friends, bosses) to let go and to give you Permission to grow up. Their job is to forgive themselves and to free themselves from their own guilty feelings. Your task is to take charge of your life and to find the parenting you need so that you can change and grow. When you forgive, you let go of your anger and resentment and instead are free to use your energy to get what you want and need to take charge of your life.

WHO'S TO BLAME?

The simple fact is that it isn't necessary to assign blame or guilt. You made the decisions you made, and blaming them on someone else doesn't change anything. If blame is to be handed out, psychologists deserve their share for promoting theories that placed the blame for so-called mental illnesses on the parents of patients. In a recent article, E. Fuller Torrey, a leading psychiatrist, created a fantasy trial where the advocates of parental blame theories were convicted and sentenced "to read and reread continuously their own writings" for a period of ten years.[2]

Permission Theory enables you to move away from assigning blame, and provides you with the tools (Permissions) to take charge of your life.

SUFFER LITTLE CHILDREN

Instead of taking advantage of the Permissions available to you, you may have made a life-style out of "suffering." You may have created your own personal variety of hell. You may have grown up believing that if you suffer enough, someone (your parents) will eventually feel sorry enough for you to give you what you want. You may also believe that suffering is a necessary part of being "grown up," an illusion you probably learned by watching other adults suffer. You may tend to seek out experiences and messages that still support your basic suffering position. You can become an expert at suffering.[3]

A mother buys her teenaged son two new shirts, and when he wears one of them the next day, she exclaims, "What's the matter? You don't like the other shirt? You are wearing the blue one instead of the green one. You never like the things I buy for you. I never can please you. I'm a failure as a mother. . . ." and on it goes.

One's natural environment certainly can be used to support hard-core suffering, or it can be used to support a satisfying, enjoyable life. Life is beautiful! The problem is that so many people just don't notice this fact.

How to Suffer	Permissions to Stay Healthy
Be stubborn.	You can ask for what you need.
Be perfect.	You can make mistakes.
Hurry up.	You can take your time.
Overadapt to others.	You can think about what you want.
Try hard.	You can do it the easy way.
Be strong.	You can feel and have needs.
Be special.	You can be yourself.
Work hard.	You can play and have fun.
Be confused.	You can think and feel at the same time.
Be stupid.	You can think and be effective.
Be inhibited.	You can be spontaneous.
Be dull.	You can be creative.
Be sick.	You can stay well.
Be righteous.	You can admit you are wrong.
Be suspicious of others.	You can trust other people.
Be tense.	You can relax and let go.

Our natural environment contains countless Permissions that many of us don't notice. When you walk down a street on a hot, humid day, do you experience the refreshment of a sudden cooling breeze, or do you continue to focus on the unpleasant humidity? Do you notice a small flower growing through a crack on a curb, or do you concentrate on the trash and litter in a gutter? The concept of figure-ground may help to explain why this happens. Look at the figure below and consider what you see.

Figure-Ground Awareness[4]

Now, look again. Do you see something else this time? Some people see the two profiles first as figures in the foreground and the rest as a ground or background. Others may see a vase first as figure and the rest as ground. It is not important which you see first. What is important is the awareness that when you are focusing on one set of perceptions there is likely another set of perceptions out of your awareness.

Your view of yourself, of other people, and of the world, can be understood in terms of what you see as figure and what you see as ground. Childhood script decisions can determine what you tend to see as figure and as ground in everyday awareness. Because of early script decisions you made, Permissions may tend to remain hidden as part of the background, and your foreground perceptions or experiences may support the negative internal messages to which you still listen.

Martha has to present a talk to the local PTA. She knows her subject quite well, but she still recalls an incident from the second grade when her teacher made fun of her in front of the class. She "listens" to the fear about appearing foolish, and as a result, she is overly anxious and gives a poor speech.

Permissions exist almost everywhere, but certain ones are usually more powerful than others. Your first step is to learn which specific Permissions you lack. This book can be valuable in helping you to discover which ones you want and need in order to change. Then you can learn how to recognize and utilize the Permissions available to you.

CLUES TO END THE BLUES

Body Cues: When you made early script decisions, you made them with your body as well as with your mind. All of your senses were involved in those decisions, so that one important way to recognize the current manifestations of the decisions is to observe what you are doing with your body.

Helen was afraid to be close to men because of some messages she heard from her mother about how "Men will have their way" and "All men are dirty." She made a decision during adolescence to avoid being close to men and to escape through books and intellectual pursuits. To insure her isolation Helen gained a lot of weight, particularly around her waist and thighs, and created a protective armor to keep men at a distance. Because she was so overweight, she was not very attractive to men, and thus felt some safety from her fears. Helen suffered from migraine headaches, which seemed to come on prior to a social outing. Helen would then feign illness and cancel her social plans. She would stay home and eat continuously attempting to dissipate her headache and feelings of anxiety.

The body stores a tremendous amount of information in the nerve endings of the muscles to help you remember the movements you once learned and now can do without thinking. Once you have learned how, driving a car or skiing are done fairly automatically. Incidents and information long forgotten are still stored in the mind and the body. As a child, when you flinched and raised one hand to protect yourself from being struck, you recorded those movements in your muscles.

Every movement, gesture, body posture, tic, or mannerism has some significance as a script signal. The way you sit, stand, walk, lie down, and breathe provides you with information about your threads to the past and the ghost messages you are still carrying around in your body. Each script signal is a thread connected in some way to some instructions you received from one or both of your parents. Awareness of this connection is the first step toward deciding which threads to sever and which to keep connected. For instance, if you are walking fast with your head slightly forward, it's likely that you are listening to "hurry up" messages, such as *"Don't be a child; hurry and grow up,"* or *"Don't be such a slowpoke."* The head tilted slightly forward can indicate a "Try hard to get ahead, but don't make it" message or a "Use your head" message. Heads tilted to one side usually are "Poor me" script signals that indicate that a person probably doesn't do much thinking and acts stupidly or "cutely" to get someone else to think for him/her.

Watching the way people sit gives you another set of script signals. Some people sit in a very closed way (*I Won't Be Close*) or in a seductive way, with legs open and genitals forward, which may also be a "Don't be close" message. A person may think he can be close physically without emotional involvement and vice versa. Also some people will look as though they are willing to get close, but as soon as someone attempts to be close to them, they get scared and back away or become rude. For example, Tina was a beautiful, petite executive secretary who moved and sat seductively. When a man would notice her and approach her while she sat in her open-legged position, she would quickly cross her legs and respond very coldly to him in an attempt to get him to go away or leave her alone. Others don't sit quietly and are constantly agitating by moving their hands, feet, head, legs, arms, mouth, etc. These movements are often signs of *I Won't Think, I Won't Feel,* or *I Won't Succeed* script decisions.

Muscle cramps often are the result of listening to "Try hard but don't succeed" messages, and chronic muscle pains can be the result of "Don't explore or discover" messages. Frowning is another signal. People with more than two frown furrows in their forehead probably use a lot of energy "trying" to think and often bury their feelings by trying to "use their heads."

Illnesses: When you become aware of the

threads that connect illnesses and early script decisions, you can begin to tune in to "early warning signals" and make other choices which can head off an illness. Sickness is also a way to suffer and make yourself weak and powerless. Illness may have been a way you got taken care of or got people to pay attention to you when you were a child. Elderly people who used this mechanism as children will tend to be sick more often when they are now feeling needy. Older and retired individuals who didn't often use illness to manipulate others when they were children, or who may have redecided to use more effective means of solving problems, are rarely sick and remain active and healthy much longer.

Verbal Cues: The words you use and the way you speak serve as definite script clues to your mystery story. If you have some resistance to accepting this point of view, it may be that you were scripted not to listen very carefully to what was said, lest you heard too much. Maybe Mother or Father wouldn't like it if you heard more than you should.

There are various kinds of verbal cues to which you may want to pay attention. Sounds themselves are important. The way you cough, sigh, grunt, cry, or laugh is tied to your past threads and to the internal messages you hear. "Gallows" laughter, or laughing at and calling attention to your mistakes or misfortunes, is a common way to replay the old script messages in your head. Saying "Boy, did I botch up that job, ha, ha!" is like saying "See how ineffectual I am—just as my parents said."

Your tone of voice has a definite tie to early script decisions you have made. If you use a parental-sounding voice, you probably are projecting your own old parental messages on others so you can feel powerful and avoid feeling the effects of the messages on yourself.

Two women were grocery shopping together. They looked to be a mother-daughter team; the daughter being in her midtwenties, and the mother in her fifties. The mother's voice, being very loud and raspy, could be heard several aisles away. She was critically evaluating her daughter, using a lot of *should*s and *ought*s and *know-better*s. She sounded very powerful and witchlike. She was projecting many ghost messages onto her daughter.

The daughter was equally loud and powerful sounding—directing many similar parent-ghost messages back at her mother.

The actual words, expressions, and slogans you use in speaking to others are examples of how you talk to yourself. If you say to others, "You should," "Why don't you?" "You've got to," or words such as "good," "bad," "stupid," "ridiculous," "wrong," or "right," you are seen by others as a bossy or controlling person. To make things worse, you probably give many of these same internal controlling messages to yourself as you attempt to keep yourself under control.[5] A myth in your consciousness may be that if you don't give yourself these messages, you may lose control of yourself and do something rash.

If you use a lot of big words and adjectives or abstract nouns, you are probably trying to impress yourself and others. If you talk about "making love" as "heterosexual intercourse," you may be treating sex too clinically in order to avoid an old parental message that "sex is dirty."

Your childlike self also has a characteristic vocabulary. If you find yourself using many *I can't*s, then you may have made some early decisions to make others responsible for you. In reality, you are saying, "I won't do it; you do it for me."

The word *but* is the universal eraser and usually means "According to my script, I would like to do that, *but* I don't have Permission," or it could mean "I don't want to do that and I don't have Permission to say 'no.'" For example, if you say, "I'll have that report to you by tomorrow morning, but I'm still waiting to get the rough draft back from the typing pool," you really mean, "I'll try hard, but I know I won't be successful."

The English language is rich in metaphors which you can use to represent your early decisions. If you see other people or things as a "pain in the butt," you may create a spastic colon as a result of your interactions. If you have a food-addiction script, you may use a number of culinary metaphors such as "I'll eat my words," "I'm in a stew about that," "Now that's a fine piece of cake," or "That's the way the cookie crumbles."

Grandiosity and miniosity (under-stating) are two ways that words can be used to support an early script decision so that internal tapes can be replayed. When you say "I'll die if I don't get a cigarette," or "You'll never be on time," you are justifying an unhealthy position in yourself or others. Grandiosities such as "I'll die if . . ." or "I'll work myself to death," or any other statements in which dying is a theme, may be threads supporting a person's *I Won't Exist* decision. Miniosities are used to call attention to something by minimizing its importance. If someone asks you, "How long have you been running a fever?" and you reply, "Only for two weeks," you are using a miniosity to support staying sick and obeying an old parental message not to take care of yourself ("Don't think" and "Don't take care of yourself").

Sweat shirt: Your body cues, illnesses, and verbal cues usually can be seen in the overall impression you give people, and are the way you present yourself to the world. This impression can be woven into a word or phrase called a "sweat shirt message." On the front of your sweat shirt usually is the message or the image you want to project, while your true feelings are contained in the message on the back of your sweat shirt. Your sweat shirt messages were usually woven from favorite slogans of your parents and represent some kind of script defense system. A parental slogan such as "What will the neighbors think?" may get translated into a sweat shirt message of "I'm a good boy" on the front, and "Ha, ha, I fooled you" on the back.

Persons with an *I Won't Exist* early decision may, in order to avoid survival fears, call considerable attention to themselves at social gatherings. They may seem to be saying "Hey, look at me," while the back of the sweat shirt reads, "I don't count." They may fear that if they are not the center of attention, they won't exist. They have trouble with lulls in the conversation, and the more scared they are that the back of their sweat shirt may show, the more they talk.

Think about what your sweat shirt message indicates on both the front and the back. As you change and grow, your sweat shirt messages will change with you.

GROWTH AND DISCOVERY ACTIVITIES

I. *The Ways I Suffer*, by _____
(your name)

Directions: Take a sheet of paper and make a list of your favorite ways of suffering.
   Examples: 1. "I like to lie on my bed, cry, and make up terrible things so I can feel bad; such as that my husband is having a torrid affair with his secretary, etc. I think of all the gory details involved in such a fantasy and feel absolutely miserable!"
   2. "I go out and buy a lot of new clothes and then I suffer and feel guilty about spending all that money for weeks afterward."

II. *Permissions I Need to End Suffering*

Directions: In looking over your suffering list in I, decide which ones you are ready to begin giving up. Think up a Permission you need to hear to change your suffering pattern.
   Examples: 1. The woman who made up bad things about her husband could begin with hearing, "You can ask for what you need from your husband, so you don't have to make up things in your head about him. For instance, ask him for several hugs tonight, or a special date doing something you really like."
   2. The person who buys clothes to feel guilty might need to hear, "You can think about what you really need in your life to feel happy. You can also think and be effective about how many clothes you can honestly afford to buy and then feel happy, not guilty, about buying them."

III. *Ways I Satisfy Myself*, by _____

Directions: On a sheet of paper make a list of your favorite ways of feeling good.
   Examples: 1. "I love to read a good book in a warm bath for as long as I wish, with no disturbances."
   2. "I love to sit under a tree in the park and watch people."

IV. *Self-Permissions*

Give yourself a pat on the back now! Tell yourself:
   I, _____ deserve to be satisfied
      (your name)
   and happy!
   I, _____, deserve to stop suffer-
      (your name)
   ing!

V. *Self-Permission Telegram*

   A. Using twenty-five words or less, write a telegram to yourself. Give yourself Permission to do something you want to do but are afraid to do. Example: "You now have my permission and support to be more effective in money matters."

_____

_____

_____

_____

B. Read the telegram to yourself and pay attention to your reaction. How do you feel receiving this telegram? What resistances do you have to doing what you have written? What are you going to do with your resistances? Example: "I felt an anger in me and a thought such as, 'Oh, yeah, just try—you'll blow it!'—I will say 'Bug off' to my head and be effective anyway."

_____

_____

_____

_____

VI. *"People Watching" for Self-Permissions*

A. Sometimes, you will discover the Permissions you want and need by watching others do things you would like to do. Check out your own reactions and see if you have Permission to do what they are doing. Make a list of things you would like to do but don't do. Example: "I would like to stand up to my boss."

_____

_____

_____

B. For each of these desires, write the internal ghost message you use to keep yourself from doing what you want to do. Example: With "I would like to swing and play in the park," the ghost message is "What will other people think of you?" _____

_____

_____

C. Now, think of what Self-Permission you can use to take the power out of your ghost message. Write a Self-Permission for each ghost message. Example: "It is fine for me to stand up for myself in the presence of my boss."

_____

_____

_____

D. Design a strategy to strengthen each of your Self-Permissions and weaken each ghost message. What you decide to do needs to be fun and easy to achieve. Example: "I will say these Permission messages ten times, three times a day, for several days, or until I think they are integrated and I believe them."_____

_____

_____

_____

_____

VII   THE MEDIUM IS THE MESSAGE

IN EVERY MAN A CHILD IS
HIDDEN THAT WANTS TO
PLAY

ECCE HOMO
—FRIEDRICH NIETZSCHE

Do and *Don't* messages are established during early childhood. We listed, in Chapter V, the earliest developmental stages at which you may have initially incorporated certain unhealthy messages. These messages form the threads for the decisions that passed through each developmental stage as you grew up. As you passed from stage to stage, you had an opportunity to examine the messages and to reinforce or change them. This recycling process goes on throughout life and is one reason some older people may seem childish. These adults don't consider alternative ways of behaving to solve a problem. They still cling to the original behavior they used to get attention or needs met as a child.

Merle was a forty-five-year-old man who still had childish temper tantrums. He screamed, ranted, and raved and stomped his feet when he didn't get his way. It was the only way he knew to act when things were not going the way he wanted. His mother used to give him his way, as a child, whenever he had a tantrum, and he expected everyone to behave as his mother had. He was in his third marriage and still acting this way and was being confronted with a possible third divorce if he didn't resolve the temper tantrums.

DOS, DON'TS, AND DEVELOPMENT

You use *Don't* messages to stop yourself from doing something that you think others don't want you to do. For example: *Don't think for yourself,* or *Don't grow up and leave me.*

A *Do* message compels you to do something (*Be*

lazy, Be stupid, etc.). Both *Don't* and *Do* messages are usually given repeatedly in a variety of forms. A smile or a frown, a spank or a hug are offered in addition to the many verbal reminders of what to do or not to do.

Don't and *Do* messages can influence your behavior in positive as well as negative ways. Most of these messages contribute to the development of healthy, safe consciousness (e.g., *Don't walk on a lake of thin ice,* or *Don't cross a street when the light is red*). In addition, all children react differently to *Don't* messages according to their own personality and makeup. Children may or may not incorporate every unhealthy message, depending upon their level of passive acceptance or active resistance. If you felt that your survival or safety depended on adaptation to a *Don't* message, you incorporated it. On the other hand, some children may decide that survival or safety exists only if they resist the *Don't* message.

Ben and Harold are identical twins; only their mother could tell them apart. Ben was the more active of the two children, and in the course of exploring was "into" everything. Harold explored too, but did so more quietly. Harold observed Ben getting his hands smacked many times a day (*Don't Explore*), and to avoid being smacked he decided not to get into the places that Ben did. Ben decided not to listen to his mother's nonverbal slapping and continued to get into trouble, while Harold listened to the *Don't Explore* message.

Safety issues may also have important influences on a child. For example, when you were a child, you may not have felt safe getting near an angry parent who projected blame onto other people. Consequently, you may have made an *I Won't Be Close* script decision.

Little Joe, a two-year-old, climbs onto his mother's lap. She exclaims in disgust, "Get down; you're too dirty, and you'll mess my dress." If she continues this action with Joe, she may teach him not to get close to her because something bad might happen.

DIRECT MESSAGES

Many verbal and nonverbal messages from parent figures (parents, relatives, teachers, etc.) are given directly to you in the process of your growing up. Even though they are given by both parent figures, the potency of opposite-sex direct messages is often greater than same-sex direct messages except in situations where a child is raised by a single parent.

Dan grew up hearing his mother say, "Don't be like your father! Get a college education and be somebody! Your brains are too good to waste." Dan decided to do what his mother said and became a research physicist and received honors for his contributions to science. We might wonder what Dan would have decided if his mother had said, "You're just like your father . . . you'll never amount to much."

Dan had a choice of following what his mother said or modeling himself after his father. His mother's messages were stronger in this situation.

INDIRECT MESSAGES

Along with direct messages, there are verbal and nonverbal messages from parent figures that are given indirectly to you. Such messages may be transmitted if you overhear your parents talking about you or about someone else. They also are transmitted nonverbally by your parents' modeling certain behaviors that correspond with the direct messages. Generally, the same-sex parent models the way in which you carry out the direct messages received from the opposite-sex parent.

Barbie overheard her father tell her mother on many occasions, "If any of our neighbors want to borrow anything from us, don't lend them a thing. You just can't trust anybody these days! They all probably have collections of things in their garages they have borrowed and never returned."

Barbie grew up believing that people were not worth trusting, as a result of hearing her parents talk. Barbie also imitated her mother's never lending things to her friends (modeling).

CULTURAL MESSAGES AND INFLUENCES

There are many other cultural threads that can influence and reinforce the basic messages and decisions you may incorporate. Television shows, films, books, plays, advertising, and schools are common cultural means for supporting script messages. Most children don't know that a culture works only because everybody believes it works and has faith that it will continue to work. There are many different cultures and they all work. If you know the concept of "cultural relativity" and know that you can survive if you change your cultural messages, then you may be able to successfully resist the powerful influences of unhealthy cultural messages. What you need to know is that if some cultural belief or message isn't working for you, you need to change it so that it does work for you.

FAIRY TALES, NURSERY RHYMES, TV, MOVIES, AND OTHER HORRORS

During your early years and as you were growing up, you heard many stories that influenced the decisions you made about what kind of person you would be. Certain characters in the stories carried meaning for you and your basic life issues (e.g., survival, suffering, passivity, needs, safety, love feelings, wants, sex, etc.)[1] Children will usually identify with a certain character in a certain story. This character then will have some important meaning for them. For example, a child who feels powerless and angry might admire the powerful and wicked Captain Hook in *Peter Pan*, or he might identify with poor, helpless Rapunzel, who wasn't allowed any needs. The *Do* and *Don't* messages given to you by your parents were intended to teach you some moral lesson.

Study Shows Western Fairy Tales Most Violent

Psychologist Doyle Gentry, head of Duke University's Division of Medical Psychology, completed a study recently showing that fairy tales read by children in Western cultures are significantly more violent than those read by children elsewhere. Dr. Gentry says Grimm's fairy tales depict twice as many acts of aggression as the Indian tales studied and four times as many as the Japanese fairy tales. "Fairy tales are important transmitters of culture found in virtually every society possessing a written heritage," he says. "They are read to children at an early age, often before the child has developed the capacity to distinguish between fiction and reality, and before he has been systematically exposed to TV and comics." Gentry said his study was conducted as part of an effort to find out why the "United States is clearly the most aggressive culture in the world."[2]

Children are exposed to a considerable amount of violence on television, and in a more limited way in the movies because they don't spend as much time at the movies. By the age of ten, the average person has spent more hours watching television than going to school. A recent survey indicates that about one half of American twelve-year-olds watch television an average of six or more hours per day. About one third of all adults watch four or more hours' of television each day.[3]

What you are exposed to on television is a world view in which justice and established authority (in their simplest forms) triumph over evil and corruption. Crises are resolved simply and quickly, and problems are solved easily and directly—usually by violent action. Much of the violence models human life as being unimportant, which is exactly the message one would get watching an evening of television. If you watch television during prime time, between eight and eleven P.M., you will receive a steady diet of violence. More than one half of all prime-time television characters use violence as their primary means of solving problems, and about one tenth use the actual death of someone as a solution.[4]

Violence on television can lead you to believe that the real world is more dangerous than it really is. This belief would support the *I Won't Explore* decisions. When asked "Can most people be trusted?" heavy television viewers were thirty-five percent more likely to reply in the negative than light television viewers. When asked to estimate their own chances of being victims of a violent crime, heavy viewers were thirty-three percent more likely to give high estimates than light viewers.[5]

In addition to teaching violence and solving problems by violence, television teaches you how to be a victim of violence. Television teaches you to accept the fact that this is a violent world in which you will be victimized. You can use your fear about the dangers of the real world to immobilize yourself, or you can cover your fear with angry cries for more use of violent action by established authority in order to control violence. It is just as irresponsible to create this distorted world view, based upon people's fears, as it is to cry "Fire!" in a crowded movie theater. Parents frequently ask their doctors about their young children's night terrors. The doctor's suggestions may be to restrict the child from watching TV for two or more weeks or until the night terrors disappear, then to select nonviolent-type shows for the child to watch thereafter. It becomes a real challenge for parents to find nonviolent shows for their children to watch.

BEHAVIORS OF PARENT FIGURES

Children's scripts become "tragic" or death oriented when parental messages are delivered with some form of severe physical or psychological punishment. Some parents are willing to threaten or beat their children into accepting and obeying *Don't* messages. Not only can the *Don't* message be unhealthy, the punishment can be a very strong reinforcement. Child abuse and infanticide often are the result of parents' desperate attempts to get their children to behave according to the parents' own unhealthy scripts.

Many parents literally have given up on their children as witnessed by a group of parents of teenagers who picketed the Gloucester County Court House in New Jersey. They demanded that the court lock up their kids. One parent said, "We want him locked up. We're begging for help, but whenever we take him to court, they just hand him back to us." Another parent has been trying for three years to get the court to crack down on her son, who she claims is unmanageable at home. She wants him placed in a psychiatric treatment center where "someone watches the doors."[6]

Some parents are operating out of many early script decisions and are not functional enough to provide for the needs of their children. Parents without grown-up, functional thinking processes have trouble getting a dog to listen to them, let alone their children.

If you had a parent or teacher who operated out of unhealthy *Don't* and *Do* messages, you may have decided it was not safe to expose yourself or risk exploration and learning (*I Won't Think* or *I Won't Explore*). Thus, one reaction would be to withdraw and adopt an unmotivated stance. Your parents or teachers may have supported their own script decisions by expecting you to overadapt to their unhealthy frames of reference.

A child in a classroom will try to please a teacher if he/she wants good grades or wants to be liked by the teacher. A teacher will sometimes single out students who are not conforming to the myth of classroom norms by making examples of these children in front of other students. Ideally, parents and teachers can provide a loving, supportive atmosphere in which children are free to make healthy decisions.

LET US SPEAK OF CHILDREN'S RIGHTS

Tens of thousands of children are severely battered or killed in the United States each year. The battering of children is not a new phenomenon to parenting. There are many historical accounts of extremes in punishment of children. Henry the VI, and Plato in 400 B.C., were among many who spoke out against the maltreatment and killing of children.

The American Humane Society, Englewood, Colorado, now has published clear information forms for all states to use as guides in reporting child abuse and neglect cases. Until these are in full use, however, in all states, many cases still go unreported or are reported inaccurately. Highlights of the 1976 National Study reported 357,533 cases of child abuse and neglect with only thirty-one fully participating states reporting. An estimated one fourth of all cases actually become statistics. If all cases were reported annually, the actual national number of abused, neglected, and killed children would be staggering.[7]

It is incredible that in our modern society of electronics and computerized homes, offices, and factories, children have been so neglected that even an efficient computerized means of reporting child neglect and abuse is still only in the beginning stages! It is encouraging that the American Humane Association is attacking the enormous problem of reporting the incident rates and the distribution patterns of battered children in the United States.

The American Humane Society has described some of the common characteristics of child neglectors and abusers.

"These are people who are losing out in life on a daily basis. They are out of step with the world. Their reality is shaded by their deprived childhood history which has left them with a lousy sense of self-value and worth. They don't like themselves and therefore are unable to trust others and form good relationships.

"Because these adults were prevented appropriate, satisfying growth as children, they have stalled at the child level. The immaturity, almost childlike pleasure seeking, impulsivity and self-centeredness is quickly noticed. Child abusers and neglectors are ill prepared to effectively deal with life in all its forms.

"They have poor perceptions of reality, make poor judgments and decisions, and live their lives in patterns of poor problem-solving, bad relationships and failures in life's tasks, like work. Their emotions illustrate anxiety, suspicion, tenseness and dependency to which they will not admit. In addition, their personal effectiveness is compounded by difficult, stressful life circumstances; for instance, poor housing, economic problems, and so on."[8]

Once we know the extent of the problem we will still be faced with the enormous task of providing solutions. Certainly, Permission Theory and its accompanying techniques can help parents and children learn to deal with the underlying causes of this terrible social problem. We know that battered children are likely to grow up and abuse their children the same way they were abused. Decisions such as *I Won't Think, I Won't Be Sane, I Won't Feel,* and *I Won't Grow Up* are common in the scripts of parents who become child abusers. Redecisions in those areas, plus learning more effective coping strategies, can help break the pattern. We can also learn to work with abused children and give them a chance to make the redecisions necessary for healthy parenting and healthy living.

GROWTH AND DISCOVERY ACTIVITIES

1. *Cultural Influences Activity*

   A. What cultural group do you belong to? Example: Middle class, Anglo-Saxon, Protestant.

   _____

   _____

   B. How long have you belonged to this group? Example: Anglo-Saxon Protestant since birth; Middle class since age ten.

C. What were the main messages you received as a child from this cultural group? Example: "Work hard now—play later."

D. What is unique about belonging to your cultural group? What are the advantages and disadvantages? Example: The freedoms and less being discriminated against, being the majority race, are advantages. The disadvantages are living a middle-class-ghetto existence.

E. As a child, how were you expected to behave with your family and with people who belonged to your cultural group? Was this different for people outside your cultural group? How? Example: "Be seen and not heard, and don't rock the boat." Somewhat different. Other cultural groups are more vocal and rebellious.

F. Did you receive special treatment because of your cultural group? How? How did this treatment affect you? Example: When a child, I think so. I could go places other cultural groups weren't approved of. It affected me by making me feel both special and angry that I was "different" from the other cultures, sort of a segregated feeling, only on my end of it.

G. As a child, were you expected to be prejudiced or "careful" with any particular group of people? Describe briefly. Example: Yes. I was told we were a superior cultural group and that others were not as smart.

H. What cultural group did your grandparents belong to? Parents? How did this affect their lives? Example: Same as A. I think they were all very prejudiced.

I. State your sex. What were you taught to do and not to do because of your sex? Would it have been different if you were of the opposite sex? How? Example: Female. I was taught to beware of men, and yet be pretty and seductive. Yes—it would have been different. I would have had more freedom and been in less trouble for being sneaky and getting caught being naughty.

J. What were the main rules in your family? Example: "Don't show the angry side of yourself." "Be trustworthy." "Have faith in yourself and toot your own horn."

K. How and by whom were you disciplined? Did you obey? If yes, how? If no, why? Example: By my mother mostly. I usually obeyed. If not, I was careful not to get caught.

L. What happened in your family when you asked questions? Example: The questions were answered. I knew some questions were not to be asked.

M. What kinds of choices did you get to make as a child? How old were you when you started making all your own decisions? Example: What I would wear.

Friends I would play with. I was age 21 when I made *all* my own decisions.

_____

_____

N. As a child growing up in your family, what did you have to do to be successful? What would have caused you to be disowned or disinherited? Example: I had to perform and excel in everything I did. I don't think I would ever be disowned for anything.

_____

_____

O. Was there a "sheep of a different color" in your family? If so, who was this person and what did she/he do to achieve this position? Example: My sister. She became independent very early in her life and joined the Peace Corps as soon as she graduated from high school.

_____

_____

P. Did you get messages about the kind of person you were supposed to marry? What were they? Example: Yes. Wealthy, professional, or famous, and social class.

_____

_____

Q. Did your family have fun together? When and how? Example: Yes. Going camping and traveling.

_____

_____

R. What do you recall was the biggest "feast day" or holiday that your family celebrated? How was it celebrated? What was your role? Example: Probably Christmas. The grandparents and relatives participated with lots of gifts and food. I helped my mother clean and cook.

_____

_____

S. What have you learned from this exercise? Example: I had a lot of expectations placed on me, and now I put a lot of expectations on myself, equally stressing.

_____

_____

II. *Do You Make Yourself Sick?*

A. What illnesses do you seem to have over and over again? Example: colds and cold sores.

_____

_____

B. Trace what happened in your life just prior to the last time you were sick. What traumas, crises, or stress-producing events occurred? Do you perceive any pattern emerging in these events as you think of other times when you were sick? Example: Yes—usually before or after a high stress time, such as a job interview.

_____

_____

C. Whom were you pleasing by making yourself sick? Example: Mother.

_____

_____

D. What internal ghost messages were you listening to? Example: "Be sick, so I can worry about you and take care of you."

_____

_____

E. What or whom were you avoiding by making yourself sick? Example: Avoiding solving a problem or doing a difficult task or expressing a negative feeling.

_____

_____

F. What internal messages did you want to avoid hearing when you made yourself sick? Example: "I'm angry!"

_____

_____

G. What did you learn from doing this exercise? Example: I get sick for a purpose.

_____

_____

VIII IT'S NOT TOO LATE TO CHANGE YOUR FATE

Decision Knots

I'VE DECIDED TO DECIDE TO
REDECIDE WHAT I DECIDED
THAT I NEEDED TO
REDECIDE, I THINK. BUT
BEFORE I REDECIDE, I NEED
TO DECIDE HOW I AM
GOING TO DECIDE TO
REDECIDE, OR ELSE
REDECIDING WILL BE A
DECISION I WILL HAVE TO
REDECIDE BEFORE I CAN
DECIDE MY REDECISION. IN
OTHER WORDS, THE
REDECISION WILL COME
AFTER I DECIDE TO
REDECIDE ABOUT MY
REDECISION. WHAT'S
KEEPING ME FROM
DECIDING IS THAT I CAN'T
DECIDE WHICH DECISION I
NEED TO DECIDE TO
REDECIDE, SO IN THE
MEANTIME I HAVE DECIDED
NOT TO DECIDE TO
REDECIDE THE ORIGINAL
DECISION UNTIL I DECIDE
TO REDECIDE THE DECISION
NOT TO DECIDE.

—THE AUTHORS

GETTING CLEAR WITH YOUR CURRENT SELF

You are basically lovable and capable. You were born that way, and at your core you remain that way. You may have made some early script decisions that have functioned to conceal your basic healthy self.

Even though early decisions were made for valid reasons, they can be changed when new information and new levels of autonomy are available.

According to Permission Theory, you have a natural drive toward restoring your basic healthy position.

RECYCLING

Cultural and social changes have made many common sex-role scripts obsolete. However, what we now know is that the natural process of human development allows us to recycle unfinished business at various times throughout our lives. This recycling process can help you to understand your own behavior and the behavior of others. A crisis, a change in your life (a move, a job change, a divorce, or a death in the family), can trigger this recycling process and give you another opportunity to redecide any early decisions and thus rewrite part of your script. Therefore, when you are dealing with a heavy, grown-up problem, you may also be dealing with related threads to unresolved childhood issues. As a grown-up, you may get angry and tell off your boss, and at the same time you may recycle two-year-old control issues you never resolved with your parents. Most people actually create situations (usually outside their awareness) in which they can legitimately recycle early unresolved problems and limiting decisions. Frank is constantly involved in romantic relationships which create problems similar to the ones he never learned to handle with his mother. Jean seems to be attracted to men who, like her father, get angry with her.

Even though you made an early script decision, you essentially get a chance to reaffirm or redecide this decision at each successive stage of your development. A desire to reevaluate is a part of a natural drive toward wholeness and completeness. When you redecide, however, you may find yourself recycling backward, clearing up the unfinished business at each stage, and finally returning to the point at which the original decision was made. For example, if you made your original decision *I Won't Exist* at age eight but made an important redecision at age twenty-five, you would also likely recycle any emancipation-stage (18–25) issues related to the early decision. You would probably recycle early adolescent and la-

60

tency issues, and you might even go back to the early oral issues related to the eight-year-old decision. Although you are not usually aware of it, the main purpose for many of your present situations is to get "unstuck" from old decisions and to make new, healthier decisions. Unfortunately, if you don't recognize and understand this recycling process and do not have the skills or information you need, you may continue to listen to old script messages and hang on to the old threads.

Stu, a thirty-eight-year-old high school graduate, rarely held a job for more than two years. He had a history of being fired or laid off or quitting his jobs. He had made an early decision not to be successful. He went into each new job with the hope of making it big and staying until retirement. However, he would consistently place his boss in a one-up power position, which coincided with his relationship with his father. In the process of recycling this power problem with his father, Stu set up situations with bosses and unconsciously hoped to resolve his original problem.

Learning to recognize the problems to recycle will give you a place to start. In order to resolve recycled problems, you will need to learn how to create a safe atmosphere in which you can get Permissions you need. Permissions are obtained from people who have clout with you and from whom you can get support for the new decision.

Below is a chart which illustrates some of the typical stages and ages wherein certain unresolved issues are usually recycled. However, there is no right time to recycle early decisions and to redecide. You can do that any time you want to.

RECYCLING CHART

Developmental Stage/Age	Issues Typically Recycled
Oral Exploratory (6–18 months)	Testing trust issues not completed in Early Oral stage
Anal (18 months–3 years)	Continuing active seeking of sensory stimulation Testing limits on exploring behavior Testing separateness
Genital (3 years–6 years)	Not thinking to solve problems (having temper tantrums, acting helpless, saying "No" but doing it anyway)
Latent (6 years–12 years)	Performing to get attention Attempting to control others in order to get attention Not thinking to solve problems ("I can't do this.") Competing for attention Exploring ways to do things
Adolescence (12 years–18 years)	Trust issues (12–13): Being sneaky Overeating (12–13): How much is too much? Testing limits (13–14): Being passive; discounting self, others, or solvability of problems Sexual identity (15–16): Acting out many sexual fantasies, having power . . . impulsiveness, sexualizing, power conflicts with opposite-sex parent
Young Adult (18 years–25 years)	Dependency issues, not asking for wants and needs to be met ("I'm not ready to grow up.") Exploratory behavior ("Who will set my limits?") Rebellion instead

Developmental Stage/Age	Issues Typically Recycled
	of thinking to solve problems
Adulthood— Creation (25 years–40 years)	Recycling with your children through their early stages of development Freedom versus control ("Who's in charge of me?") Dependence relationships, "drifter syndrome" ("I can't settle down")
Adulthood— Reevaluation (40 years–60 years)	Rebellion against growing old (45-year-old teenager) Discounting social commitments ("I wish I were a kid again.") Exploring outside of earlier established limits
Adulthood— Resolution (60+ years)	Dependence issues Overeating and self-indulgence instead of seeking attention from others Hassling about rules Suffering rather than thinking

Your task is not to become script free, which would mean you have no life plan with which to organize what you say and do. Your task is to update and change your script. Making this change means you can take charge of your life and reclaim your birthright: *The Right to Be Lovable and Capable.*

WHY SCRIPTS RUN OUT

It was easier for your parents and grandparents to make early script decisions around a basic life plan and to carry that script with them to their death. If your mother's script was grounded in her role as a mother, she shifted her focus only slightly to preserve her role as she became a "grandma" who still had child-care responsibilities and who worried and "fussed" over her children and grandchildren living nearby. Shifting her position became more difficult when her children moved two thousand miles away after high school or college and started their own families away. Lack of family proximity, combined with value changes concerning the role of women in our society and the modern conveniences which make housework less demanding, has left many women holding on to the end of a very short script thread. One woman put it this way: "I woke up one day at age thirty and found that my goals of being married and having kids, a house, and a successful husband had been met. Then came the frightening thought: What am I going to do with the rest of my life?"

Having your script run out can be a frightening experience if you are not prepared for it. In reality, if you know that this is a normal part of human development and are prepared for it, you can turn that scare into excitement and begin to write a new script for yourself when you need to or want to.

REWRITING THE SCRIPT

Owing to the rapidly changing nature of modern society, you need to reevaluate and update your basic life decisions more often than before. In a changing world, not to change is to become obsolete. Rigid, stereotypic values have limited utility in the midst of a values revolution. You are living in the greatest period of social and cultural change in all of recorded history. This requires constant reexamination of information, attitudes, and beliefs. For example, ninety percent of all the scientists who ever lived are still alive today. This fact alone has led to incredible scientific discoveries. In most scientific areas, the data base (that which people know to be true) has turned over completely during the past ten to twelve years.[1]

In addition, people are on the move more than ever before, which indicates the temporary nature of modern society. Every year since 1948, one out of five Americans has changed residences. Of the 885,000 listings in the 1969 Washington, D.C., telephone book, more than half were new listings.[2] Currently, it is estimated that one out of three American families will move each year. Employment is also in a state of flux. The day is gone when someone stays with a single career for a lifetime. Many people now change jobs and careers six, seven, even ten times during their working years. Obviously, with as much transience built into everyday life, the stability of an extended family (grandparents, aunts, uncles, cousins) and a stable group of close friends probably isn't possible for you. These conditions constantly force you to reexamine your information, attitudes, values, and beliefs. Permissions and redecisions are a vital part of healthy living.

WE CAN'T STRESS THIS TOO MUCH

With so much of your life in transition, you will have to deal with stress as a way of life. One of the obvious effects of change and its attendant stress is in the breakdown of the family. The National Center for Health Statistics reports that within the United States in 1976, there were 2,126,000 marriages and 1,026,000 divorces, with a divorce rate of 4.8 per 1000 population. By contrast, in 1965, there were 1,800,000 marriages, 479,000 divorces, and a divorce rate of 2.5 per 1000.[3]

Chronic stress can make you ill if you let it. Some stress is necessary in life, but too much is harmful. You could be falling victim to the Great American sickness called "hurry up!" The simplest remedy to this stress producer is to learn how to take your time and take care of yourself emotionally and physically. There is a variety of antistress training programs available, including meditation, self-hypnosis, biofeedback, yoga, centering, acupuncture, massage, martial arts (such as tai chi or aikido), and physical conditioning. Less esoteric methods include taking naps or siestas, maintaining good eating and sleeping habits, and being good to yourself on a regular basis.

It is sometimes hard to get good data on cause-and-effect relationships regarding psychological factors and illness. For example, does cancer cause smoking or does smoking cause cancer? Stress is no exception to this dilemma. We do know that there is a clear relationship between stress and illness; but at present not enough is known about cause-and-effect factors. Some work has been done in the classification of personality types, the use of stress within those personality types, and the resultant development of heart disease and cancer.

Two pioneer medical practitioners, Carl and Stephanie Simonton, at Cancer Counseling and Research Center, in Fort Worth, Texas, are developing revolutionary methods for successfully treating certain cancers. They are using meditation and visualization techniques. They have patients imagine their white blood cells killing the cancer cells, and they show them slides of other patients who have been cured. The Simontons have patients read *The Will to Live* by Dr. Arnold Hutschnecker; they tell patients, "You can cure yourself if you believe you can," along with administering standard radiation therapy.

In addition to these revolutionary techniques, they have begun to isolate various personality traits and related factors associated with the disease. Their findings indicate that the biggest predisposing factor to the development of the disease is the loss of an important love object occurring six to eighteen months prior to the diagnosis. The predisposing personality characteristics they found most clearly associated with the disease are a tendency to hang on to resentments, a refusal to forgive others, a tendency toward self-pity and suffering, little ability to make and keep meaningful, long-term relationships, and a very low self-image. In a two-year study, the Simontons report that between ten and twenty percent of their patients who were diagnosed incurable now show no evidence of disease.[4] This evidence would at least begin to suggest that giving yourself certain kinds of cancer may be tied into various script decisions in some way. For example, it could be the manifestation of an *I Won't Exist* or an *I Won't Have Needs of My Own* decision.

People do tend to make themselves sick when there is a "payoff" for being sick. When you don't want to do something that you think you should do, you may try to avoid it by making yourself ill.

> Bob was a restaurant owner who learned that on the following Monday he would have to close his establishment and dismiss the employees. Over the weekend, he came down with a severe case of laryngitis, so bad that his doctor ordered him to bed. This illness may have been Bob's way of avoiding an unpleasant situation. In the meantime Bob solicited the help of his accountant in dismissing the employees.

DEGREE OF INVESTMENT IN THE DECISION

When you invest in stocks and bonds, real estate, or a savings account, you expect a certain return on your investment. You may decide to invest a little in a number of different securities or stocks, or you may put all your money into one investment. So it is with script decisions. When people invest a part of themselves in a decision, they expect a return for their investment. As we said earlier, your decisions are made to turn over responsibility for some aspect of your life to others, and the return you hope for is that others will handle this responsibility to your satisfaction. You expect a definite return on your investment, and you can put considerable energy into protecting and guaranteeing a return, particularly if you carry your investment from childhood to adulthood. The longer you have had the investment, the more energy you might be willing to put into protecting it. People who have invested in having their parents or society be responsible for them and take care of them in important areas of their life will often go to rather desperate lengths to maintain their investment.

Some people may have a heavy investment in certain early decisions and a lighter investment in others. Generally, a light investment in a decision is seen in people's social behavior. They may play certain social-level games and limit their happiness, success, or effectiveness.

Jerry goes to a cocktail party given by his boss. He wants to make a good impression, but he is afraid of making a mistake. His boss walks up and asks "What'll you have, Jer?" Jerry suddenly can't think of what he "should" order, so he says, "Oh, nothing; I'm not hungry, eh . . . I mean, thirsty right now." Jerry realizes that he surely didn't make the good impression he wanted to make.

At the second-degree level of investment, there is more covert and concealed behavior. Much of the action at this level is internal. Obsessive thoughts about real or imagined problems or dangers can consume considerable time and energy. Depressions occur at this level of investment and may affect eating, sleeping, working and other daily routines. People invested at this level may appear distant or detached a good part of the time.

After fumbling the ball on the drink order, Jerry begins to worry about what his boss must think of him. He sees his boss talking to others and imagines he is telling them about his clumsy behavior. Jerry withdraws further and feels unsafe. He decides to leave, makes some excuse about feeling ill, and goes home feeling miserable.

The third-degree investment usually involves doing tissue damage, either to self or to others. This level usually affects all areas of a person's life. Chronic alcoholism, drug addiction, criminal behavior, or chronic psychosis are common symptoms.

Jerry finds all social situations very scary and avoids them. He has no friends and escapes social contact by sleeping. Because he refuses to socialize, people begin to ignore him. One night in a drunken, depressed state, Jerry kills himself by driving his car into a bridge abutment.

BANAL SCRIPTING

If your early decisions are affecting only selected areas of your life (first- and second-degree investment), you may have what is called a "banal" script, or a script that goes nowhere. These are common cultural or family scripts based upon roles and role expectations. As a woman, you may have a banal script which directs your role as "the woman behind the man." You stay out of the spotlight and allow your husband to receive public credit. Behind the scenes you actually run the whole operation, but hardly anyone knows it. A common banal script for a male in our culture is that of "playboy," in which a man chases after the perfect woman who doesn't exist. He has very stereotypic views of relationships, based mostly upon what he sees on TV, in the movies, in comic books, or in popular pulp magazines. A playboy script doesn't allow enough intimacy to develop to have relationships.

COMMON BANAL SCRIPT THEMES[5]

Women	Ghost messages	Script Decisions
Mother Hubbard	You don't deserve any better. You're not important. Be nice to others. Know your place. Sacrifice for your family. Be a good helper.	I won't have needs of my own. I won't think (outside of the home). I won't exist.
The Woman Behind the Man	Be seen and not heard. You shouldn't have been a girl. You're not as important as a man. You don't deserve any better.	I won't feel. I won't have needs of my own. I won't be the sex I am.
Plastic Woman	Be cute. Don't be natural. Don't change.	I won't grow up. I won't feel.
Poor Little Me	You'll never amount to anything. Others should know what you want. Don't be important. Don't do anything right. Other people will take care of you.	I won't think. I won't grow up. I won't succeed.
Creeping Beauty	Don't like yourself. Beauty is only skin deep.	I won't be close. I won't feel. I won't have needs of my own.
Nurse	You're not important. Take care of others. Know your place. Work hard (suffer).	I won't have needs of my own. I won't feel. I won't be close. I won't be a child.
Fat Woman	Don't like yourself. You don't deserve any better. You'll never amount to anything. Don't change.	I won't feel. I won't be close. I won't think. I won't exist.
Teacher	Help others. Don't make waves. You don't deserve any better. Be independent.	I won't have needs of my own. I won't feel. I won't be close. I won't be a child.

Women	Ghost Messages	Script Decisions
Guerilla Witch	Don't trust others. Be tough. Be scary. You are special.	I won't be close. I won't be me. I won't be sane.
Tough Lady	Be strong. Men are stupid. People can't be trusted.	I won't be me. I won't be close. I won't feel. I won't be a child.

Men	Ghost Messages	Script Decisions
Big Daddy	Be in control. Take care of others. Be strong. Never admit weakness.	I won't feel. I won't be close. I won't be a child. I won't have needs of my own.
The Man in Front of the Woman	Try hard. You'll never amount to anything. Someone will always help you. You can't do it right.	I won't succeed. I won't exist.
Playboy	Women are objects. Don't be real. Don't change. Be cute. You deserve more. Don't give yourself away.	I won't grow up. I won't be close. I won't be sane.
Jock	Be strong. Watch out for others. Try hard.	I won't think I won't feel. I won't grow up. I won't be close.
Intellectual	Use your head. Be in control. Be right. Others are stupid.	I won't feel. I won't be a child. I won't be close. I won't be the sex I am.
Woman Hater	Women can't be trusted. Be in control. Keep your distance. Be tough.	I won't get close. I won't feel.

When early decisions affect major areas of your life (third-degree investment), you may act out a tragic or harmful script. When a person ends up dead, injured, or institutionalized, it is a clear indication of a third-degree investment. A skid-row drunk or a hardened criminal may be acting out a tragic script.

Most people's early script decisions seem to cluster around three basic script patterns: a discount script, a deprivation script, and a drug addiction script. The following chart identifies early script decisions that fall under each of these patterns.

THREE CLUSTERS OF SCRIPT DECISIONS

Discount Script Decisions	Deprivation Script Decisions	Drug Addiction Script Decisions
I won't be close.	I won't think.	I won't feel.
I won't have needs of my own.	I won't succeed.	I won't be a child.
I won't be the sex I am.	I won't grow up.	I won't exist.
	I won't be sane.	I won't.

You have a *deprivation script* if you fear that there isn't enough of what you want to go around, and that you are going to be deprived of whatever you define as scarce. You may have decided that you have to compete to get your share, but that you probably will not get it. This is an angry position where you are still trying to blame someone (most likely your parents) because you can't get what you want. You are constantly comparing yourself with others to see if you are winning or losing.

"Stroke" is a word used to describe a verbal or nonverbal unit of attention. There are societal myths about a scarcity of strokes and love ("There isn't enough of what I want and need to go around"; "You have to manipulate and control others to get them to give you strokes"). These myths provide a major arena wherein you act out your deprivation script decisions. If you have invested in this script, you may need Permission to ask for strokes, to accept strokes, to offer strokes to others, to reject strokes you don't want, and to give yourself strokes.

A *discount script* consists of your decision not to think and not to solve problems for yourself.

This involves your discounting your feelings, your abilities to think, and your capacity to solve problems. The decision is "I won't, so you will have to." You may also discount other people, the existence of problems, and the importance or significance of a problem. If you manifest these behaviors, you need to start being accountable for your behaviors and being responsible for thinking and for solving problems. This means you will have to stop blaming others and begin to remember to do the things you need to do to be responsible.

> Susan was ten and had certain jobs she was expected to do around the house. Instead of doing the task during her free time, she would wait until bedtime. For instance, suddenly she would remember she hadn't fed her guinea pig and then be angry at her mother for putting her to bed. Susan thought it was her mother's fault that the guinea pig didn't get fed. She would say, "If you didn't make me go to bed, I could feed my guinea pig." Her mother would say, "Susan, you have had all afternoon to feed your guinea pig. It is your responsibility to get your jobs done. Now it is your bedtime."

The *drug addiction script* is, in reality, a nonfeeling script in which you have severed your connections with your feelings and from your body. You may have drugged yourself with alcohol or drugs to block or escape certain thoughts and feelings. You may need to engage in deep breathing exercises to help reestablish contact with your feelings and your body. Deep breathing activities can help you to reconnect yourself with your feelings.

You may find that your early decisions encompass all three basic script patterns to some degree, but that one of the patterns is predominant.

The timing of an early decision varies considerably. For banal scripts, a decision may not be made until late adolescence, while tragic script decisions are often made quite early. Many people can remember a single incident when they actually made a decision.

> Sondra, a frail four-year-old, was crossing a shaky bridge with her mother. Sondra had poor balance and coordination and slipped and fell into the river. Sondra's father was quickly summoned to rescue her. Sondra was angry with her mother for not protecting her on the bridge, but she thought her mother would not under-

stand or accept her anger. To compensate for her fear of expressing anger, Sondra developed asthma because asthma was acceptable and safe, while expressing anger was not (I Won't Feel).

GROWTH AND DISCOVERY ACTIVITY

I. *Script Ledger*

Below is a script ledger. On one side you can list the amount of investment you have made in each of the eleven evil script decisions and what you hoped or still hope to get in return. Example: "I won't succeed." Decision: First-degree. Return: "People will treat me specially and won't expect as much from me."

Decision and Amount of Investment	Expected Return on Investment
1.	
2.	
3.	
4.	
5.	
6.	
7.	
8.	
9.	
10.	
11.	

II. *Body Problems*

A. Close your eyes and think about a body problem with which you are currently dealing. Toss the problem around in your mind for a minute or two, and pay attention to the various thoughts and messages connected with the problem.

B. Now, keeping your eyes focused on the problem, locate the problem in your body. Where do you experience the problem in your body? Pay attention to what happens to your body as you focus on that part of the body where the problem resides. Now, breathe about four or five strong, deep breaths into the problem spot in your body. Allow the problem to move out of that spot and spread throughout your body. Keep breathing and exhaling completely each time. With each exhalation, feel the problem moving out of your

body until you don't feel it anymore. Now send yourself loving messages about taking care of your body and your problems. Example: "You are a neat person because you deal effectively with your body and your problem."

III. *Space Perimeter*

A space perimeter is like an imaginary wall around you. To discover your space perimeter, do the following: Find a partner, face each other about four to six feet apart, and maintain eye contact. Walk toward each other, slowly, until you feel uncomfortable. The instant that you feel uncomfortable say, "Stop," and have the other person stand still. The distance between the two of you denotes the amount of distance you need to feel safe and comfortable with this person. This is your body space perimeter. Everyone has a different perimeter, and people growing up in different cultures have different perimeters. Your perimeter will vary with different people too. Try this with a member of the opposite sex and with someone of the same sex. What differences do you notice? Whom do you keep farther away, men or women? Reverse roles and learn about other people's external body space perimeter.

IV. *Body Blocks*

A. Stand up and close your eyes. Now, place your hand or hands over the part of your body that you dislike the most and wish you could cover or hide.

B. Discuss this with a partner or a group of people. Share your feelings about that part of your body and get feedback from others. Try to remember any messages connected with why you dislike that part of your body.

C. Now, stand again with eyes closed and cover the same disliked part. This time, think loving thoughts about that part of your body and love yourself for having negative thoughts and feelings about it. This is a sometimes difficult but necessary part of self-acceptance.

V. *Taking Care of Your Body*

A. Write one thing you are not doing to take proper care of your body. Example: *Not exercising.*

B. Whom are you pleasing by not taking care of your body? Example: *My Father.*

C. What negative messages are you listening to or avoiding listening to when you do not take care of your body? Example: *"You're lazy!"*

D. Ask for a Permission message from your partner or another person to take care of your body: "It's fine for you to_____
_____."

E. Give yourself a Permission message to take care of your body: "It's fine for me to_____."

F. What are you going to do to take better care of your body? "I am going to _____ and _____."

IX   DECISIONS, DECISIONS, DECISIONS

THE HARDEST THING TO
LEARN IN LIFE IS WHICH
BRIDGE TO CROSS AND
WHICH TO BURN.

PETER'S QUOTATIONS
—DAVID RUSSELL

REDECISIONS

You have now begun the process of unraveling the mysteries about yourself, about the *Don't* and *Do* messages that influenced your early decisions, and about the consequences of these decisions. You are beginning to be aware of the origins of your feelings and behaviors.

You may reach a point of impasse, a stuck spot, where you actually sense a danger in going further and you also know there is no turning back. The stuck spot may be related to a fantasy of your parents' rage if you changed the original decision and disobeyed their command. A person may equate loss of love and nurturing support with giving up the early decision. You may blow up or magnify the images of your parents' power. When you place your parents' power in proper perspective, you will see yourself as having more power and clout.

If you feel stuck, you may need additional assistance to go ahead and redecide the original decision. You can seek support through group or individual therapy or from a person or persons to whom you have given clout. This support may be necessary at times to help you reduce the power of the *Don't*s and *Do*'s. Resolution of the impasse is prerequisite for change.

Although giving up old decisions may be scary, hanging on to them and staying in a stuck position is even scarier.

Getting out of an old script and acquiring a new sense of self-worth is similar to a butterfly emerging from an old cocoon with straight wings that fly. Fantasize that butterfly staying stuck in its cocoon—a dilemma, yes?

Feeling stuck is not hopeless; it is a dilemma that stimulates you to change. You are totally in charge of where you are now, where you are going, and how you are going. You are in charge of your own strength. If you are stuck and remain stuck, it is because you have decided to stay stuck. You can redecide to get unstuck. This is what a redecision really is: Giving yourself Permission to take charge of yourself!

THE MYSTERY OF THE INVULNERABLES

The principal of the elementary school explained that Tom had everything going against him. He counted the strikes against Tom: ". . . extreme poverty, an ex-convict father who was dying of a chronic disease, an illiterate mother who sometimes abused him, two mentally retarded siblings." The principal continued, "Yet his teachers described him as a charming boy, loved by everyone in the school, a good student, and a natural leader."

A research group at the University of Minnesota, headed by psychology professor Norman Garmezy, is studying case histories of children who, despite their parenting and environmental conditions, have developed healthy coping skills. In trying to explain this unpredictable phenomenon, the professor said, "They bounce back! They just have a tough bite on life." Then he added cautiously, "What its roots are, I don't know yet."

He hopes his research will help determine how these "invulnerables" make it. He hopes to find out . . . "not just how they survive in difficult circumstances, but what it is that makes them thrive."[1]

In Permission Therapy this phenomenon is explained as the result of an early script decision not to blame others for your life situation, and a decision to take charge of your own life. What looks like a highly unusual example may be quite common, but because of the emphasis on negative parental and societal influences it is often overlooked. People do make decisions and redecisions in childhood if the circumstances require them to do so. But for many people these redecisions (or decisions to take charge of their life) don't occur until adulthood, if then.

COMMON SCRIPT MYTHS

Many of your early decisions may be tied to cultural myths created through collective misinformation. The following chart lists some of the common script myths that people have reportedly believed. Check to see how many of these you still believe. *Think about and incorporate the Myth-Breaker Permission messages that will enable you to redecide and to use the Redecision Structure effectively.*

COMMON SCRIPT MYTHS CHART

Myth	Myth-Breaker Permission
I can cause thoughts and feelings to occur in other people. ("I'm sorry I hurt you.") ("You made me angry.")	I am responsible for my thoughts and feelings, and other people are responsible for theirs.
I have the power to make others lovable and capable.	Each person is in charge of her/his lovableness and capableness. I can't control or determine this for another person.
There was only one slot for me in my family when I was growing up ("I'm the cute one; she's the smart one").	I may have believed that when I was growing up, but now I can decide to be who I want to be.
I can trick or manipulate others into caring for me or loving me.	Others care for me or love me because they choose to and because they find me to be lovable.
If other people really cared, they would anticipate my needs and wants.	I am the only person responsible for seeing that my wants and needs are met.
Asking for the strokes I want and need is being pushy and self-centered.	Asking for the attention I want and need is the most effective way to take care of myself.
The world should be fair—according to my rules of "fairness."	The world does not operate according to my definitions or my rules. What I need to do is to decide how I want to live, according to the rules that exist.
I am special.	I have no right to expect special attention from other people. I am unique in many ways and not special in any way. (See page 72)
There are not enough of the strokes I want and need to go around (scarcity myth).	There is no limit to the supply of attention available to me.
I will be bragging if I think or say positive things about myself.	Loving myself and liking what I say is an important part of choosing to be lovable and capable.
If I accept positive strokes I want from others, they will think I am conceited.	Accepting attention I want is an important way to take care of myself.
If I don't notice something, it can't affect me (discounting problems).	Taking good care of myself involves noticing those things that are important and accounting for them in solving problems.
If I anticipate the worst that could happen, then it won't happen.	I can't control the future. What I can do is account for what is happening and likely to happen as a consequence of my behavior.
I have to do something before I can get the strokes I want	I deserve attention because I am me, and I don't have to do something to

Myth	Myth-Breaker Permission
(performance myth).	"earn" the attention I want.
I don't deserve to get what I want because 1. I'm not lovable and capable, 2. I'm not perfect, or 3. I'm _____ .	I can get what I want because I am lovable and capable.
People will think I am rude and inconsiderate if I don't accept strokes I don't want.	I am in charge of deciding what attention I want and need and what attention I don't want or need.

I'M SPECIAL, HOW ABOUT YOU?

Many people grow up believing an *I Am Special* myth. The threads of this myth are found in the *special* symbiotic relationship you had with your mother during the first eighteen months to two years of life. Nature protects you by creating a mutual dependency between mother and child. This relationship begins to change as you venture to explore and to solve problems on your own. If, as in many families, the symbiosis is not resolved completely as you grow up, then you will hang on to a myth that you have to be special to someone else and that someone else has special attention just for you. The core issue with specialness is rooted in your beliefs that there isn't enough love for you and you must compete with others to get your share. In some cases, this issue has survival feelings attached to it because, in the original form, survival was an issue.

As you grow up, you may reinforce the myth by entertaining fantasies about your power to control your mother or father to insure that you will get the special strokes you need. This fantasy likely starts during the magic years (three to six) and continues into latency and adolescence. If it isn't redecided by then, it is usually carried into adulthood. As adults, we often carry out the myth by marrying someone who will treat us as special and someone whom we fantasize we can control to insure a continual supply of special strokes.

There are cultural influences that help promote the myth. The heavy cultural messages about being good parents help promote control and guilt-invoking behaviors on the part of parents and children. For children, this is translated into "I'm going to control my parents (a fantasy) to give me the special treatment that I once had and still need." Parents, on the other hand, are often afraid of rejection if they don't try to give their children special strokes. This control mechanism also operates between a husband and wife to avoid rejection.

Further cultural influences come from the "Be special" messages we give men and women. Men are taught that they are special by birth alone and through constant cultural messages. For example, most men have been taught that because they are special, they deserve to get more strokes or attention from a woman than they give in return. For women, it is very different. They have to overcome the original sin of being born female, and the way to do this is to treat a man as special and hope that he will validate her and therefore make her special to him.

I'M MORE SPECIAL THAN YOU ARE!

The *I Am Special* myth creates an arena in which comparative and competitive thinking have a field day. Since special strokes are limited in quantity, you had better protect your supply. This myth leads people to watch each other carefully, to make sure that certain people don't give away too many special strokes to others. Couples attempt to control each other and constantly monitor each other's behavior to make sure they are getting enough special strokes. Each wants to make sure the other person hasn't decided to give his or her special strokes to someone else. Relinquishing this special-stroke myth is an essential part of redeciding many early script decisions.

Once you have freed yourself from believing that anyone can possess specialness, you can begin to see how you are unique, and how other people are unique also. In addition, since you have no need to place strokes in "special" categories, you are more free to give and receive strokes straight, with no strings attached.

In relationships, it is only through the surrendering of this myth and forgiveness that we can really see each other as separate, autonomous, and unique individuals. It enables people who have been married or living together for twenty, thirty, or forty years to get to know each other for the first time. It is sad when you maintain a barrier that prevents you from really knowing others whom you love and who can give love in unlimited quantities. Love is one of the basic human qualities, and when you give love freely, you find your own supply is unlimited.

THE PERMISSION CHART

The Permission chart presents a way of organizing Permissions so you can learn how to give and receive Permissions in many different ways. Permissions are available almost everywhere. Below are some common forms of Permission messages.

1. *A direct verbal Permission* is a message given (in words) directly to you or by you to another person. You have direct eye contact with another person, as well as that person's complete attention or awareness of you and the situation.

Meredith, aged six, went to the park to play with her classmates. When she sat on a bench and didn't join the others in rolling down the hill, her teacher asked why she was sitting alone. Meredith replied, "I'm afraid I will get a grass stain on my clothes, and my mother will be mad" (*I Won't Be a Child* decision).

The teacher then looked Meredith in the eye and said, "It's fine for you to roll down the hill with the other children. If you get a stain, it will wash out. If your mother is angry, I'll be glad to discuss it with her."

Meredith happily joined the class in rolling down the hill. The teacher may have had to give Meredith's mother Permission to allow her daughter to be a child ("Children get dirty").

2. *A direct nonverbal Permission* is a direct message given without words. Since about ninety percent of our communication is nonverbal, many potent messages are given and received in this manner.

A mother was proudly telling her friends, "I have my children so well trained that all I have to do is snap my fingers when I want them to stop what they are doing. I don't even have to say a word" (a nonverbal *Don't* message).

In changing script messages, direct nonverbal Permissions are potent ways to say, "I care about you." Hugs, strokes, back rubs, touches, smiles, eye contact, kisses, and play are such expressions of caring.

3. *An indirect verbal Permission* is a message given verbally, in your presence, to someone else. You hear the message and can think about how it might work for you. You may imagine trying on the Permission in your own life and situation. You may recall the message later when you are in a situation that calls for a change of thinking or responding.

Young Jim hated to take out the trash during "his week." His younger sister Joyce also hated this chore during "her week." Joyce overheard Jim complain to his mother, "I hate having to take out the trash again." His mother replied, "You don't have to like it, but you can still do it."

The next week Joyce said to herself, "I hate this, but I don't have to like it to do it." She had already incorporated an indirect verbal message that she could use for herself, although it was given to Jim.

4. *An indirect nonverbal Permission* is watching or experiencing someone else doing something nonverbally that you would like to do but don't have Permission to do.

Two businessmen were on their lunch hour and decided to "brown bag" it in the park on a picnic table. They both were looking secretly at the swings and wishing they could swing, but neither had Self-Permission to "let their kids out." They noticed that two other men, also in business suits, began to swing. After they had eaten their lunch, one of them said, "That looks like fun. If those two men wearing ties can swing, so can we. Come on, let's do it!"

The other man could hardly wait, and beat his friend in a footrace to the swings. If those other men hadn't come to swing, these first two probably wouldn't have found the indirect nonverbal Permission to swing and to have fun.

PERMISSION CHART

	Verbal	Nonverbal
Direct	"You can _____."	Nonverbal Permission strokes.
Indirect	Hearing someone else receive a verbal message giving a Permission.	Observing others doing what you may want to do but don't have Permission to do.

THE REDECISION STRUCTURE

The following Redecision Structure is designed with change in mind. It is a framework to use when making a redecision. It will aid you in clearly thinking through the thoughts and feelings necessary to make a real redecision. It can also be used for other redecisions not listed in the book.

Since I, _____ , decided that _____
(your name)   (original decision)

_____ ,

I _____ will now redecide that _____
(your name)   (new decision)

_____ .

What I'll get out of this is _____
(Positive consequence)

_____ ,

and I, _____ . will _____
(your name)

_____ .
(self-permission)

Example:

Since I, _____ , decided that *I Won't Have Needs of My Own* I, _____ , will now redecide that *I will be effective in getting my needs met.* What I'll get out of this is *self-worth* and I, _____ , will feel better about myself.

In Chapter XV, *Using Permissions to Change Your Life Decisions,* you will be able to use the Permission Chart and the Redecision Structure to prepare yourself for actual redecisions. The Growth and Discovery Activities at the end of this chapter also provide you with additional information to use in making new decisions about who you want to be.

GROWTH AND DISCOVERY ACTIVITIES

I. *Permission Awareness Activities*

  A. Direct Verbal Permissions
    1. Give someone a direct verbal Permission. For instance, if one of your friends or colleagues comes to you and says, "I don't know what to do about this problem," you can respond with, "It is fine for you to think how to solve it."
    2. Ask someone for a direct verbal Permission. For example, plan to do something you have always wanted to do but didn't have Permission to do (e.g., buying and eating a banana split deluxe). Tell your friend your plan, ask him/her to tell you, "It is fine for you to do what you need to do." Then go do it!
    3. Give yourself a direct verbal Permission (follow-up of #2). Tell yourself, and/or look in a mirror.

  B. *Direct Nonverbal Permissions*
    1. Give someone a direct nonverbal Permission. Let someone know you support and care about him/her. This can be accomplished through a smile, a touch, a positive look, a hug, etc.
    2. Ask someone for a direct nonverbal Permission. Or smile at yourself in a mirror, for example.

  C. *Indirect Verbal Permissions*
    1. By your giving someone a direct verbal Permission in the presence of someone else, you may be giving the bystander an indirect verbal Permission. Later, this may be noticeable in the bystander's reactions or change in behavior.
    2. Listen when someone gives a direct verbal Permission to another person. Think about how this message might apply to you. Try it on for size. Recall it later and apply it to a situation in which it might work.
    3. If you have a tape recorder, record five verbal Permissions meant for yourself. First say them as if you were speaking to someone else, then say them as if you were speaking to yourself. Example: "It is fine for you to feel angry about _____ " then, "I can feel angry about _____ ." Replay the Permissions several times and really listen. You are giving yourself indirect verbal Permissions. Remember to listen to yourself.

  D. *Indirect Nonverbal Permissions*
    1. When others watch you give another person a direct nonverbal Permission, they also experience it. You are indirectly giving the bystander Permission to do what you have Permission to do. Be aware of others observing your Permissions.
    2. Watch others giving nonverbal Permissions. Stay alert to your own reactions and see if you have Permission to do what they are doing. If

not, consider what may be blocking you.

3. Give yourself Permission to work through any blocks on the preceding pages.

4. Give yourself Permission to do a lot of people watching for indirect non-verbal Permissions. Pay attention to those Permissions you observe and use the ones that apply to your own situation.

II. *Redecision Exercises*

A. *Fantasy of the Future.* Fill in the blanks:

1. Where will you be five years from now if you don't redecide and change your present life script?

_____

2. Where will you be five years from now if you change your life script?

_____

3. Where will you be ten years from now if you don't redecide and change your present life script?

_____

4. Where will you be ten years from now if you change your life script?

_____

B. *Fill in the Blanks:*
Example:
I used to _____
  (cry when I was angry)
but now I _____
  (express my anger appropriately)

1. I used to _____
   but now I _____

2. I used to _____
   but now I _____

3. I used to _____
   but now I _____

C. *Permission Telegrams*
Using twenty-five words or less, write a telegram giving Permission to someone to do something you know he/she wants or needs to do but won't do. _____

_____

_____

_____

2. What would you imagine his/her reaction would be if you actually sent this telegram? How would you want him/her to react? _____

_____

_____

_____

_____

III. *The* I Am Special *Myth-breaker*

A. Complete the sentences listed below with the myths you believe about yourself. Example: "I am special because *I am very good-looking.*"

1. I am special because _____.

2. I am special because _____.

3. I am special because _____.

4. I am special because _____.

5. I am special because _____.

6. I am special because _____.

7. I am special because _____.

8. I am special because _____.

9. I am special because _____.

10. I am special because _____.

B. Think about and list what you would do differently if you were no longer special in each area you listed above. Example: "I don't deserve any special treatment based on my looks."
   1.
   2.
   3.
   4.
   5.
   6.
   7.
   8.
   9.
   10.

C. Now, make a list of all the "special" people in your life. Rank order them in importance to you. Opposite their names, list the ways in which they are special to you.
Example: Wife: Cooks delicious meals. Great sex partner. Intelligent. Understanding.
Rank   Special Person
Ways Person Is Special to You

_____

_____

_____

_____

_____

_____

D. Now, complete the sentences below with the "special" expectations you may have of others. Example: "Because I am special, I expect *others to read my mind.*"

1. *Because I am special, I expect* _____

_____

2. Because I am special, I expect _____

_____

3. Because I am special, I expect _____

4. Because I am special, I expect _____

_____

5. Because I am special, I expect _____

_____

E. Describe below how you will get what you want and need without thinking you are special and without controlling or manipulating others into a "special" relationship with you. Example: "I will ask for what I want, instead of expecting others to read my mind."

1. _____
2. _____
3. _____
4. _____
5. _____

SECTION TWO

TECHNIQUES
FOR
CHANGE AND GROWTH

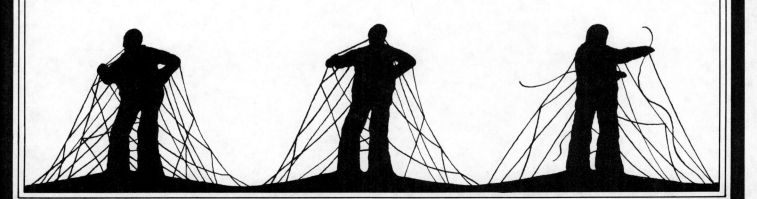

X HOW TO UNRAVEL YOUR MYSTERIES

THE UNFORTUNATE THING
ABOUT THIS WORLD IS
THAT GOOD HABITS ARE SO
MUCH EASIER TO GIVE UP
THAN BAD ONES.
A WRITER'S NOTEBOOK
—SOMERSET MAUGHAM

OVERVIEW OF TECHNIQUES FOR CHANGE AND GROWTH

In Section One, you learned the basic principles of Permission Theory. In this section, you will learn how to use the techniques of Permission Theory and grow as a person. Presented in this section are the three basic and three advanced techniques that use the principles of Permission Theory and show you how to change old habits and to learn new ways of thinking, feeling, and behaving.

The basic techniques begin with learning to forgive your parents for not giving you everything you wanted and needed while growing up. As was said earlier, learning to forgive your parents is fundamental to all other change processes. By forgiving your parents you can make it possible for yourself to learn how to get the Permissions you still want and need from others. This is the second basic technique. Finally, you can learn how to make use of Self-Permissions to change and grow.

The advanced techniques build upon the basic ones and provide you with additional tools for change and growth. These six techniques are presented to you in a step-by-step manner so you can practice and learn how to apply the principles of Permission Theory.

PROCESS VERSUS PRODUCT LEARNING

If you encounter some initial difficulty in learning these six techniques, it may be because you have been accustomed to product learning and not process learning. Most schools and colleges still place a heavy emphasis on learning content and facts as product rewards. Yet in a rapidly changing world, what is true today may not be true tomorrow. To deal effectively with personal growth and change, you will have to learn processes rather than facts. You will have to learn how to learn, unlearn, and relearn, and then apply this kind of learning to any content or facts.

Much of this book is concerned with process learning. The information in the book helps explain various life processes, and the skills and techniques are designed to help you better manage and cope with these life processes. Each of the six techniques for applying Permission Theory involves learning a process which, once learned, can be applied to many situations and problems.

BEING IN TRANSITION

Sometimes one of the hardest parts of change and growth is learning to live comfortably in transition. You may have let go of old and familiar patterns of behavior and you may have not developed firm new patterns to replace what you changed. Every person who has changed, even if it's just a hairstyle, has had to face some anxiety about the effects of this change. Each time you let go and take the leap into the unknown, you will get better at handling the transition.

It is sometimes helpful if you can begin to chart your progress through the misty never-never land of transition. There are at least three identifiable stages of transition. The first stage of transition involves being aware that you are breaking away from an old pattern of behavior. During this stage your thoughts and efforts are directed at avoiding the old patterns. You still have vivid images of the ill effects of the way you used to be, and are hoping by constant vigil that you will stay clear of them. There is usually considerable fear that you may return to the old, if you are not careful.

Stage two involves establishing a solid beachhead in the middle ground between what was and what could be. There is a clear awareness of where you are going, but there is no momentum in either direction. You are no longer avoiding the old, but you haven't begun to seek the new very actively. The onset of this stage is usually marked by the realization that you have taken some irreversible steps and you can't turn back. There is usually an equal amount of fear and excitement attached to the realization that you are simply *in transition*.

Stage three, or the resolution stage, involves a clear focus on the newly emerging pattern of behavior. Very little energy is used to look back to old patterns or to experience being caught in the middle. There is more excitement than fear at this stage, and each new step increases this excitement.

One way to chart your own course through these stages is to first identify how much of your energy and attention is focused on each stage. Try the following experiment. Choose an aspect of yourself that you are actively involved in changing. Write down three statements: 1. I am in transition *from* something, 2. I am in transition, and 3. I am in transition *toward* something. Then assign a percentage to each category that represents the amount of time and energy you spend in each. The sum of the three percentages should equal 100%. For example, you might rate yourself: In transition *from 60%*; *in* transition *30%*; and in transition *to 10%*. This would indicate that you see yourself involved mostly in breaking away from an old pattern and are just beginning to realize that you are in transition.

A THREE-STAGE MODEL OF CHANGE AND GROWTH

There is a predictable process of change and growth that can be broken down into three stages. The first stage usually involves an increasing awareness that your life is not working well in certain areas and that the information and thoughts you are listening to are not helping you. If you have not forgiven your parents, either symbolically or directly, you may be recycling guilt-resentment programs, etc. You may still be trying to get what you want from your parents (or parent substitutes) by pushing harder on their guilty button. You may finally realize that you can't get what you want from other people by trying to make them feel guilty. Your parents may not be willing or able to give you everything you want and need now. If you decide to forgive your parents, then you are free to move on and get parenting from other sources where the information and Permissions are readily available.

When you have decided to give up your attach-ments to ghost messages from your past, then you will begin looking for new sources of information and Permissions. These sources could be a book like this one or another person. The person could be an old friend, a trusted teacher, a therapist, a boss or co-worker, or someone else who seems to have what you need and want. These sources or persons become natural authorities in the areas of your life in which you wish to change and grow. Natural authority, or clout, is based upon recognized expertise, knowledge, experience, and willingness to respond authentically and respectfully to others.

A person with those qualities also serves as an important form of protection during an early stage of change and growth. A person who has clout often is seen and heard by you as saying, "Listen to what I say or do about this; don't listen to those internal ghost messages anymore." Protection or support comes from regular contact, over a period of time, during which you receive the information and Permission messages you need and want. During this time, you are in the process of testing out your new information and Permissions. Maintaining regular contact also helps you to resist reverting back to listening to your ghost messages again. The protection and support also help you to resist scaring yourself while you are learning to do and say things you once thought were forbidden.

This first stage of the change and growth process can take fifteen minutes, five months, or five years. The length of time depends upon you and how long you have decided to take. It also depends upon how important it is for you to change or not change. You may watch from a distance for months before deciding to give another person clout. The following exchange may be part of that testing period.

> Student: Do you think I am smart? I don't think so.
> Teacher: Sure you are! And if you decide to believe it, you will be even smarter.

Stage two, the expansion stage, involves an expansion of the first stage process. During the first stage, the emphasis was on finding new sources of information, Permissions, and support. Now the emphasis is on expanding the search to include other sources. Having only one source can lead to unhealthy dependence and possibly a restoration of an old symbiotic attachment. A client may say to her/his therapist, "Gee, Doctor, I don't know what I would do if I couldn't see you every week." The therapist who doesn't confront that statement may be using the situation to recycle her/

his need to have people dependent upon her/him.

It is important for you to know there are many sources of information and Permissions for you. Movement through the expansion stage is aided by finding and/or establishing support groups or using natural systems to help you solidify your new information and Permissions. A consciousness-raising group, a therapy group, a work team, or some group of people with whom you interact on a regular basis is helpful during this stage. For example, if you wish to give up suffering, it is helpful to have a group of people you can meet with regularly who also are giving up suffering. They can explore with you new ways to structure your time and interactions together. At first, you may have to create this support for yourself because it may not exist in your natural environment. You may be surprised to find that some of your friends are invested in supporting your ghost messages because they have chosen you to support their complementary messages. Changing your messages and behaviors may require you to change your friends as well. Also, you may find new support systems by changing jobs and joining new clubs and organizations in which there are more people willing to support your changes.

Stage three, the internalization stage, emphasizes an internal source of Permission, clout, and support. You no longer need as much external support and are now able to manage your change and growth more independently and interdependently. Permissions also take on a new meaning during this stage. You can now give yourself Permissions, trust yourself to listen to your own Permissions, and act appropriately on them.

The change and growth process nears completion when you can take in the new information and Permissions, decide to use them, and then obtain validation from yourself and others for acting effectively in new ways: "It's OK for me/you to be close to others." The process is finalized when you no longer act on the ghost message, but rather you act on the new information and Permissions. You may still be aware of the presence of old ghost messages, but their power and influence is reduced to the point that you no longer feel compelled to act on them.

Being successful in changing one area of your life may lead you to venture into other areas. You can use this part of a natural growth-discovery process to reach heights within yourself you never thought possible!

XI   FORGIVING YOUR PARENTS

TO FORGIVE IS MERELY TO
REMEMBER ONLY THE
LOVING THOUGHTS YOU
GAVE IN THE PAST, AND
THOSE THAT WERE GIVEN
YOU. ALL THE REST MUST BE
FORGOTTEN.

THE COURSE IN MIRACLES

BASIC TECHNIQUE #1
THE ART OF GROWING UP

Your childhood script decisions were made to make your parents and others responsible (to blame) for various aspects of your life. You, like most people, may be hanging on to some anger and resentment toward others (parents and parent substitutes) because certain aspects of your life are not as successful as you would like. Unless you are willing to forgive your parents, *you will not grow up* and take charge of your life. Forgiveness is basic to all change and growth.[1] Forgiveness means giving up your resentment against your parents and giving up your desire to punish them in some way. Though this technique is basic, it is often one of the most difficult to learn. Take your time unraveling the threads connected to blaming others for your shortcomings or failures. If you get confused or stuck on any part, put the book down for a minute and relax; give yourself Permission to be effective at learning this technique. If you are still stuck, go back and reread parts of Section One and complete more of the Growth and Discovery Activities at the ends of the chapters.

The method you choose for forgiving your parents is entirely up to you. You may choose symbolic methods (without communicating directly with them). For example, since the resentment is your creation, regardless of the amount of suffering you may have had as a result of something your parents did to you, you can let go of that resentment without ever communicating it directly to your parents. You may also choose direct methods of forgiveness. A rule of thumb we have found useful is that if you can forgive symbolical-

ly, then you can also forgive directly, if your parents are still alive. Be sure that the direct approach does not have some secret desire to punish them. Remember that the act of forgiveness is for your benefit and not theirs.

The forgiveness process has the following stages:

1. Forgiving your parents (symbolically or directly).
2. Forgiving yourself.
3. Giving up all claims to punishment of your parents and yourself.
4. Releasing your parents and yourself from your previous relationship.
5. Restoring a harmonious relationship with your parents and yourself.

STAGE ONE:
SYMBOLIC PROCEDURE

Rationale: In stage one, forgiving your parents, it is important to remember that *forgiveness becomes the "master erase."* Only after you have forgiven your parents can you let go of old resentments and negative thoughts. What remains then are the positive loving thoughts that had been there all the time and which were masked by your resentments. The main reason for forgiveness, however, is that everything not forgiven by you will continue to repeat itself in your current relationships.

Step One: Find yourself a quiet place where you will not be interrupted for about a half hour or more. In the spaces below write down your thoughts and feelings about your parents.

_____

_____

_____

_____

_____

_____

_____

_____

_____

Step Two: Identify which parent you are focusing on. Then head the list, "I resent you because . . ." writing as many resentments as you can remember.

Example:
"I resent you because you never told me you loved me."

_____

_____

_____

_____

_____

_____

_____

_____

_____

Step Three: Again, identify the parent upon whom you are focusing the procedure. At the top of the list write, "I appreciate you because . . ." writing as many appreciations as possible.

Example:
"I appreciate you because you taught me to value honesty."

_____

_____

_____

_____

_____

_____

_____

Step Four: Again, identify the parent upon whom you are focusing. Draw a vertical line down the middle of a new page. Then write at the top of the left-hand column the following open-ended forgiveness Permission: "I forgive you for . . ." Then at the top of the right-hand column write, "I am still resisting forgiving you because . . ." Go back to your list of resentments and use them to complete this step. See how many resentments you are willing to convert into forgiveness. Continue this process until you can't write any more resistance statements.

Example:

| "I now forgive you for . . . not telling me you loved me because I know you never could do that." "I now forgive you for not always knowing what I wanted or needed." "I now forgive you for not being perfect." | "I am still resisting forgiving you because . . . that is bullshit. You should have known I wanted to know I was loved." |

_____

_____

_____

_____

_____

_____

_____

_____

_____

If you are resisting doing this exercise, you probably are not ready to forgive your parents in those areas in which you are experiencing resistance. First, go to those areas in which you were able to forgive. Even if you have only one solid forgiveness, you can build on that one. Some people complete this process in one sitting, while others may take years to get completely through the forgiveness process. Second, look at the areas in which you still have resistances and identify some Permissions you need for dissolving the resistance. For example, if you are still blaming your parents for not telling you that they loved you, think about some Permissions or other information that might help you forgive them. List at least three things you do to dissolve the resistance. Example: Find out how many other people your age had similar experiences and find out how they have handled the situation.

VARIATIONS OF THE SYMBOLIC PROCEDURE

Some people can complete the forgiveness process by writing a letter to each of their parents (without sending it) that expresses their resentments, appreciations, and forgiveness. Another variation involves acting out the process. If you have a partner who is willing to assist you, you can use pillows or chairs to represent your parents; you can even engage in a dialogue with them by exchanging pillows or chairs. Your partner can take notes and monitor you for any nonverbal resistances. If you have a group of people, you can have various people play your parents, and through role reversal you can show the players how you believe your parents would react. With the help of a trained facilitator, this can be a beneficial experience for the whole group.

DIRECT PROCEDURE

Again, keep in mind while using a direct approach that you are forgiving your parents for yourself and not for them. If you are going to deal directly with your parents, you probably will need to make clear to them why you are forgiving them. However, it is likely that if you have hung on to resentments and guilt for some time, then possibly they, too, may not have forgiven themselves. The task of self-forgiveness is theirs, not yours. If you are going to use a direct face-to-face approach, it is important to allow sufficient uninterrupted time. However, you do not have to finish in one sitting, and you may prefer to space out the time.

VARIATIONS OF THE DIRECT PROCEDURE

Writing a letter and sending it to each of your parents is another way to complete this process. Perhaps you can write a series of letters back and forth if you are separated by some distance. You can also telephone or mail a tape recording.

STAGE TWO: FORGIVING YOURSELF

Rationale: The process of forgiveness only begins with your parents. The next step is to forgive yourself for blaming others and not being strong enough to take responsibility for your life. This part of forgiveness is attainable only after you have let go of your old resentments toward your parents. Even so, it can still be a formidable barrier to overcome. Forgiving your parents allows you to give up the illusions you have held on to about yourself and others, and allows you to see yourself as you really are. For some this is a large dose of reality and may be difficult to swallow at first. You may fear that since your parents are no longer to blame for your misery and suffering, then you must be. The truth is that blame has nothing to do with it *and it never did*. Blame is an illusion, something that you invented and that never had any reality, except in your mind. So when you forgive you can also let go of the illusion of blame.

The following procedure can help you understand your relationship with yourself more fully and enable you to move on to the other techniques for using Permission Theory.

Step One: Find yourself a quiet place where you will not be interrupted for a period of time.

Step Two: On the left side of the paper write the following self-forgiveness Permission: "I now forgive myself for all my mistakes and offenses against myself." On the right side of the paper write any resistant thoughts you have about that self-forgiveness statement. Rewrite each resistance on the right into another self-forgiveness statement on the left.

Example:
"I now forgive   "I have been such a
myself for all my   fool."
mistakes for which
I suffered."
"I now forgive my
foolish behaviors."

_____

_____

_____

_____

_____

_____

_____

_____
_____
_____

STAGE THREE:
GIVING UP ALL CLAIMS TO PUNISHMENT

Rationale: Now, even though you have forgiven your parents and yourself, it is important to make sure you have cleansed yourself of all claims to punishment. Punishment for a mistake seems only natural and is the mechanism for holding on to resentment. It is therefore essential that all urges for punishment be removed. The following steps will help you process out any hidden thoughts of resentment and punishment.

Step One: Again sit down in a quiet place where you will not be interrupted for a period of time. Draw a vertical line down the middle of the lines below.

Step Two: At the top of the list identify which parent you are focusing upon. Then write the following Permission in the left-hand column: "I now give up all claims to punishing you for _____ ." In the right-hand column write any resistances that emerge. Change any resistances into positive messages on the right side of the page.

Example:
"I now give up all claims to punishing you for not telling me you loved me."
"I now acknowledge my love for you and yours for me."

"I haven't wanted to tell you that I love you."

_____
_____
_____
_____
_____
_____

Repeat this process, perhaps referring back to the resentment list for further clues to possible punishment urges. Once you write these statements without resistance, you have probably cleared them from your consciousness. After you have done this with each parent, then do it for yourself, ridding yourself of any self-punishment urges.

STAGE FOUR:
RELEASING YOUR PARENTS AND YOURSELF

Rationale: This stage enables you to let go of any illusions you may have about controlling your own behavior or the behavior of others. You may have had a strong attachment to the "old" relationship with your parents and with yourself. This stage is designed to help you release the "old" attachments or thought processes you may have.

Step One: Find a quiet place where you will not be interrupted for a period of time. Draw a vertical line down the middle of the lines below.

Step Two: In the left-hand column write the following release Permission: "I now fully and freely release my (mother, father, etc.) to find her/his highest good in her/his own way." Then in the right-hand column write down any resistances that surface. Change each resistance into a more specific release Permission.

Example:
"I now fully and freely release my mother to find her highest good in her own way."
"I now fully and freely release my mother from her anger to find her highest good in her own way."

"She is too angry."

_____
_____
_____
_____

_____

_____

_____

_____

_____

_____

Repeat this process with each parent until you are satisfied that you have let go of any control illusions. Then do the same process on yourself. Write the following Self-Permission: "I release myself from all illusions of control and acknowledge that I can find my highest good in my own way."

_____

_____

_____

_____

_____

_____

_____

_____

STAGE FIVE: RESTORING HARMONY

Rationale: This stage is designed to help you further support your new relationship with yourself and your parents. Expressing appreciations and gratitudes is an important part of this stage. What seems to be true is that you cannot be grateful and resentful at the same time.

Step One: This time starting with yourself, make a list of things you appreciate about yourself and are grateful for in yourself. Again divide the paper vertically and bring to the surface any remaining resistances.

Example:
"I appreciate my   "You sound vain."
sense of humor."
"I am grateful for
my good looks."
"I appreciate my
sensitivity to
myself."

_____

_____

_____

_____

_____

_____

Step Two: Now do the same process with each of your parents. Write all the things that you appreciate about each of them and all the things you are grateful for in your relationship with them.

Step Three: Take all of the expressions of gratitude and appreciations toward your parents and write them in a letter to each parent. Send a letter to each of them separately. It is important to put them in writing because they seem to have meaning when done in this way.

_____

_____

_____

_____

_____

_____

_____

_____

Step Four: Now write a letter to yourself expressing all the gratitudes and appreciations you can muster for yourself. Mail the letter to yourself so you can experience receiving it in the mail.

_____

_____

_____

_____

_____

_____

_____

_____

_____

All of these stages are part of a healing process for you and for your parents. Once you have completed this process you will have restored harmony to your life and have a clear pathway to engineer your life the way you want it to be. No longer do you have to feel stuck in old patterns or old resentments. If you feel yourself getting stuck again, simply use this process or parts of it to clear the barriers you have erected and move on.

HOW OTHERS HAVE USED THIS TECHNIQUE

Example #1

Shirley was depressed much of the time. She felt life was not worth living and that she was powerless to change her situation. Occasionally, she would get extremely angry and lash out at her husband and two small children for some minor reason. Then she would feel guilty and become even more depressed.

In therapy Shirley received many Permissions to express anger, and she received information about expressing anger in appropriate ways. Gradually, over several months, Shirley began to identify anger and resentment toward her father and mother. For years she had secretly been blaming them for not outwardly demonstrating love for her while she was growing up. She realized she had begun feeling depressed when she was a child. She now saw that her depression represented an attempt to make her parents feel guilty and pay attention to her. She also realized she still did this not only with her parents but also with her husband and her children. However, she now clearly perceived that she had other options to help her to get what she wanted. Instead of trying to manipulate and control others with her old mechanism—depression—Shirley decided, after receiving Permissions, to forgive her parents and focus her energy toward getting the love in healthier ways.

Example #2

Lucy had all the outward signs of success. She was very attractive and pleasant, was married to a successful businessman, had lovely children and was active in civic organizations. She also had a successful career as a teacher. Inside, she felt empty because she allowed her mother to control her life. She was "required" to visit her mother every week and talk with her on the telephone almost daily. Her mother evaluated everything Lucy did and told her what to do and not to do. Lucy resented this control but was willing to let her mother take charge. In this way, Lucy could always blame her mother for anything that went wrong. She also tended to allow herself to be manipulated by her husband.

Because of the Permissions and support she received from a weekly therapy group, Lucy finally got the courage to confront her mother directly. She scheduled a full morning with her mother and she began to express her resentments and appreciations. She met with her mother on numerous other occasions. Finally, Lucy was able to forgive her mother and take charge of her own life.

In her therapy group, Lucy reported increased energy, liking herself more, getting along better with her husband, and experiencing an equal, sharing relationship with her mother.

XII USING PERMISSIONS FROM OTHERS TO UNRAVEL YOUR MYSTERIES

THERE IS AS MUCH
DIFFERENCE BETWEEN US
AND OURSELVES AS
BETWEEN US AND OTHERS.
ESSAYS, VOL. I
—MICHEL DE MONTAIGNE

PERMISSIONS ARE WHERE YOU FIND THEM

After you have freed yourself from the negative energy spiral by forgiving your parents, you can begin to use your energy to find the information and Permissions you require. This usually means finding a source (such as this book) or another person who's a natural authority for you. A natural authority is a source of information and Permissions that you decide to listen to instead of listening to your childhood script messages. After you make the difficult decision to find the Permissions you want or need, the finding itself is often surprisingly easy.

Maria returned home to live with her mother after finishing college. At the same time she came to a therapy session with one of the authors. She said, "I wasn't sure why I wanted to move back here with my mother, but I knew it was important. Now I know why and I'd like to join one of your therapy groups." During the first meeting of the therapy group, she said to the group, "I came back to this city to complete some unfinished things with my mother. When I complete them, I will be moving on."

At her second weekly group session, she received a number of Permissions from me to do what she was ready to do. In that session, she was able to express anger and resentment toward her mother and to decide to forgive her mother for not providing all she wanted and needed.

Two days after this session, she called me and said, "I have finished what I came here to do, and now it is time for me to get

on with my life. I am leaving to find a job in California. Thank you for your help and support."

SUPPORT IS WHERE YOU FIND IT

Very often the sources of information and Permissions have been there all the time—you just didn't notice them before. One of the important parts of change and growth is building a supportive environment for the changes. It is likely you have structured your life to support your internal ghost messages rather than the new Permissions. You choose friends, activities, hobbies, and interests to support your beliefs. If you want to change, you may need to restructure your life to support these changes. You may need to find new friends or make new supportive agreements with old friends, find new hobbies and activities. One man reported to a friend that he was going to sell his stamp collection, which had taken almost twenty years to build, because he realized he had used the collection to stay away from people for a long period of time. Instead, he took ballroom dancing lessons and joined a toastmasters' club.

Look at how you spend your time and examine how you may be hanging on to threads from your past in the form of childhood script decisions. A good way to do this is to keep track of how you spend your time during a day—or a week, if necessary. Keep a twenty-four-hour time chart and then go back and see how many things you did that were *have to*s and how many were *choose to*s. (Example: "I have to go to work," or "I choose to go to work.") Those things that you are defining as *have to*s are probably the threads connected to childhood script decisions. You are behaving as if someone were making you do that activity instead of your deciding or choosing for yourself.

Some things that are really *choose to*s can still be supporting old decisions. Ask yourself, "What could I be doing instead, that I would enjoy doing more?" Make yourself a list of thirty things you really like to do. Then ask yourself, "When was the last time I did each of these?" Aside from seasonal aspects (skiing in the summer is difficult), these are the things that you need to plan to do if you have not done any of them in a while. Take some time to think about how you are going to restructure your life to support your change and growth.

PERMISSIONS IN THE NATURAL ENVIRONMENT

As you begin to restructure your life, you will open yourself to Permissions that were there all the time. Everyday events may take on new meanings. You may suddenly discover natural Permissions and support coming from people you haven't noticed, from books, music, art, and just everyday experiences. You may notice a flower growing out of a crack in a sidewalk or the rhythmic chant of the subway noises. People may begin to see you differently, too. People at work may say, "You know, there's something different about you lately; I don't know what it is but I certainly like it."

BUILDING A SUPPORT SYSTEM FOR CHANGE

There are a number of ways to build an organized support system for yourself. Consciousness-raising groups have been used by many women to get the Permissions they wanted and needed. More men and couples are using this kind of support group to break out of banal script messages. These groups can vary greatly, from political action groups to more personal-action ones. They can provide a place where you can discover that other people have similar issues and problems, and learn how they deal with their problems. Knowing you are not alone in what you are experiencing can provide important support and Permission. A good reference for how to establish a consciousness-raising group is *The New Assertive Woman* by L. Z. Bloom, et al. (Dell, 1976).

Many of your friends and co-workers would be willing to support you in your changes if you asked them. (Example: "I want to share my feelings more with you. Is that all right with you?")

Your spouse and/or intimate friends can represent an important source of support for change. It is important to make them part of your changes so they don't scare themselves unduly about how you are going to change the way you will relate to them. In your excitement, you may not notice signs of their fear at first. In relationships where unhealthy forms of dependency are present, a person's initial decision to change may stir up more feelings than expected in a partner. Many dependency patterns are imbedded in day-to-day activities, so change will require that you develop contracts with your partner. For example, a usual dependency pattern involves one person's doing something because the other person can't do it (e.g., cooking meals). In exchange, the other person does something his/her partner can't do (e.g., paying the bills and balancing the bank statement). A healthy agreement could involve each person agreeing to teach the other the skills he/she has that the other person doesn't yet have. Then the sharing of everyday chores can become more cooperative and less competitive.

Therapy, too, can be used as an important source of support. Many therapists have good information and Permissions you can use to support your changes. Not all therapists are willing to function as natural authorities, so you may need to do some shopping until you find the one for you.[1]

Group therapy can function as a temporary support system while you are organizing a more complete system. Group therapy, similarly to consciousness-raising groups, provides you with the awareness that others have similar problems and concerns as well as providing a variety of models for solving problems.

BASIC TECHNIQUE #2: ASKING FOR PERMISSIONS FROM OTHERS

Rationale: Learning how to ask for what you want and need seems very simple. However, most people have trouble asking directly for what they want, and instead tend to be indirect and somewhat manipulative. Some Permissions will come your way without your having to ask for them, and some won't. Learning and using this skill will increase your chances of getting what you want and need.

Step One—Identifying Permissions: The first step is to know what specific Permissions you want and need. If you are having trouble identifying them, refer back to the Growth and Discovery Activity #1, Messages and Permissions, at the end of Chapter III. If you haven't done so, complete that activity and then make a list of Permissions you are now lacking.

Step Two—Asking for Permissions: To practice this skill, find a partner who has clout with you. Join hands with this person and look directly into his/her eyes asking the following questions:

Question: "Will you give me Permission to _____?"
Answer: "Yes, you can _____."

Example: "Will you give me Permission to *do what I need to do, even though I am scared?*"
"Yes, you can *do what you need to do to take good care of yourself even though you are scared.*"

Partners need to monitor any nonverbal signs on your part that indicate you are not letting in the Permission. Some people break eye contact or stop breathing to keep themselves from receiving the full impact of the Permission. You may resist Permissions at first because you know letting them in means letting go of the old ghost messages.

Step Three—Getting What You Want: Repeat the above process with each Permission you still want until you have completed your list. If you do not like the way your partner expresses your Permission, ask him/her to rephrase it. Also, in both the question and answer, keep the language very simple. A good rule of thumb is to use words that an eight-year-old would understand.

Step Four—Supportive Permissions: Still holding hands and facing your partner, say the following: "What I am going to do with this Permission is _____. Will you give me supportive Permission to _____?" Your partner answers, "Yes, I support you in doing _____." or "Yes, you can _____."

Example: "What I am going to do with this Permission is *ask my husband to spend more time with me.* Will you give me supportive Permission to *ask my husband to spend more time with me?*"
"Yes, I support your *asking for what you want from your husband.*"

In this step, the Permissions are more specific and are related to taking some action on the Permissions given previously in steps Two and Three. Repeat this step with as many Permissions as you are ready to act upon.

VARIATION OF BASIC TECHNIQUE #2

Step One—Thinking and Feeling: Make a list of all the Permissions you want and need. After each one, record the basic feelings that are associated with that Permission. The five basic feelings are fear, anger, sadness, happiness, and excitement. You should be able to identify at least one basic feeling for each Permission, and some Permissions will have several feelings connected with them.

Step Two—Asking for Permission: Again, to practice this skill find a partner who has clout with you. Join hands with this person and look directly into her/his eyes, saying the following: "I am _____ (basic feeling) about _____, and what I want from you is _____ (permission). Will you give me that?" Your partner answers, "Yes, you can _____."

Example: "I am *scared* about *asking my husband to spend more time with me,* and what I want from you is *Permission to do what I want even though I am scared.* Will you give me that?"
"Yes, you can *ask for what you want from your husband even though you are scared.*"

Repeat this process with each Permission you want.

HOW OTHERS HAVE ASKED FOR PERMISSIONS

Example #1

Eric, age twenty-nine, was a member of a men's consciousness-raising group. One night he announced to the other men in the group that he was going to give up listening to his internal messages that "real men don't cry." After the group, he experienced an overwhelming sense of despair. He visited his closest friend, Ted, who was also a member of the group, to talk about his despair. Eric realized that the despair was connected to another childhood message that "change brings on suffering." He asked his friend to give him Permission to make changes without suffering. Ted said, "Sure, you can ask me or any of the other people you know to give you Permissions and support."

Example #2

Thirty-four-year-old Marie came to her therapy group with a specific problem. She said, "I hate it when my husband touches and caresses me. I usually want to avoid having sex with him because I have to allow him to touch me. When we do have sex, I want to get it over with as quickly as possible."

When asked what she thought was the origin of this feeling, she said, "My mother and father never touched me and I never saw them touch each other." She had realized that she had decided at a very young age there was something wrong with her and that was why no one touched her. This belief was now causing her serious marital problems. Marie needed numerous Permissions to change this belief and find out she was worthy of being touched. Marie agreed to ask each week for a hug from a group member. At first this was very difficult for Marie, but gradually she allowed herself to enjoy it. Finally, one night she asked the whole group to give her a back rub. She said, "I now know I am important enough to get all the touching I want." At a later meeting she reported spending an hour making love with her husband and really enjoying it.

XIII GIVING YOURSELF PERMISSIONS TO UNRAVEL YOUR MYSTERIES

SELF-TRUST IS THE FIRST
SECRET OF SUCCESS.
SOCIETY AND SOLITUDE:
SUCCESS—
RALPH WALDO EMERSON

HOW TO BELIEVE IN YOUR SELFNESS

Many people have strong, contaminating messages about being selfish. For some people, the worst thing anyone can say to them is "You are selfish." Many religious values emphasize being unselfish as a goal. Between selfish and unselfish, there is a third position: *selfness*. This is an act of loving, caring for, and believing in yourself.[1] This middle ground is often overlooked because of all the confusing rhetoric about selfish and unselfish. Actually, selfness is where you reside most of the time, anyway. You just learn not to let others know about your selfness, lest they mistake it for being selfish. Selfishness means meeting your own needs at someone else's expense and should not be confused with selfness.

Selfness is:
—Taking care of yourself instead of manipulating others to do it.
—Choosing for yourself instead of having others choose for you.
—Respecting your rights and others'.
—Setting your own goals responsibly and working to achieve them.
—Feeling good being with yourself.
—Being satisfied with yourself and forgiving yourself.
—Giving strokes willingly to others (asking directly for strokes when needing them).
—Making clear your values and beliefs but not imposing them on others.
—Giving positive Permissions to yourself.
—Becoming your own nurturing inner parent.
—Letting in love and affection from others.
—Being yourself when with others.
—Sharing your thoughts and feelings with others.

—Being willing to "own" your own thoughts and feelings and not blaming others.

If you are open about your selfness, some people may react with anger and fear, but most people will respect and like you for respecting yourself.

HOW TO NURTURE YOURSELF

Most people do not know how to nurture themselves. It is a skill, and like any other skill, it can be learned. If you were to make lists of all the things you like and dislike about yourself, which list would be longer? If you are like most people, your "dislike" list would be much longer than your "like" list. When was the last time you did something good for yourself? When was the last time you told yourself what you liked and loved about yourself? When was the last time you made love to yourself? When was the last time you took yourself out for a night on the town? These activities might seem strange and alien to you, and if they do, you probably need to learn how to nurture yourself more than you now do. Your capacity to love another person cannot be greater than your ability to love yourself. Also, you cannot accept any more love from others than you are willing to give yourself. It takes courage to love yourself and express your selfness because you are risking being authentic. You may block your selfness because you fear that others will misunderstand, judge, critically evaluate, and even reject you. The courage to express selfness openly comes from caring more about what *you* think of yourself than about what *other* people think of you.

BLOCKS TO SELF-NURTURING

One of the main blocks to expressing your selfness is the common cultural myth that you are capable of *causing* the feelings, thoughts, or behaviors of others. Statements such as "You made me angry," or "You made me miss my bus," support the myth. In reality, everyone chooses his own reaction, and you can't control how someone else will react for you. You can control only your own reactions! Due to this myth, you may believe you can't take care of your own needs because they may cause someone a problem. *You alone are in charge of yourself!* Give yourself the following Myth-Breaking Permission: "I am responsible for my thoughts and feelings and other people are responsible for theirs." Repeat this to yourself and let it sink in. If you really care about yourself, you will not let anyone else take responsibility for anything that belongs to you. Also, you won't take responsibility for anything that belongs to anyone else. Remember, this does not mean you are selfish and disrespectful of the rights and privileges of others; it means you are offering them your highest respect.

BASIC TECHNIQUE #3: GIVING YOURSELF PERMISSIONS

Rationale: Your most important task is to replace the internal ghost messages with healthy, positive Permissions. This means that you have to learn new ways of talking and listening to yourself. Learning to internalize the Permission process is essential so that you can replace the ghost messages, rewrite your script, redecide, and stay current with yourself. Several different programmed activities follow, to help you learn this valuable technique.

SELF-PERMISSION ACTIVITY #1

Step One—Mirror, Mirror, on the Wall: Take one minute a day, look at yourself in a full-length mirror, and say five positive, nurturing things to yourself. Say them as if you were speaking to another person (e.g., "You are pretty," etc). While you do this, notice any blocks or resistances you may have. Do you tense up parts of your body? Do you begin to hear "Yes, but . . ." messages? Do you qualify your statements? ("You are pretty when you dress up?")

Step Two—Building a Self-Permission List: Keep a log of the positive Self-Permissions you give yourself each day. Say and record a new set of five each day until you have at least a hundred different, positive Self-Permissions recorded in your log. After you have your list, go back and repeat the ones you had the most difficulty giving

yourself or the ones that were the most powerful.

Step Three—Living Your Self-Permissions: Part of the process of changing the way you talk and listen to yourself involves conscious practice in using Self-Permissions each day. You may want to write some of the most important ones on small cards and carry them with you. Using your Permissions, you can make posters and have them around your house. Take your favorite, most important Self-Permissions and dictate them into a cassette recorder. Play back those Self-Permissions while you are driving your car or before you go to bed at night. All these suggestions will work if you really want to become more comfortable with your selfness.

Step Four—Acting on Your Self-Permissions: The most important step is using your Self-Permissions to do things you previously would not have done because you were listening to your internal ghost messages. Use the following format to write and/or say what you are going to do.

"Because I am ＿＿＿＿＿＿ today, I'm
(positive Self-Permission)
going to ＿＿＿＿＿＿
(new behavior)
instead of ＿＿＿＿＿＿ ."
(old behavior)

Example: "Because I am *fun to be with* today, I'm going to *ask someone new to go to lunch with me* instead *of eating lunch alone or with the same people.*"

SELF-PERMISSION ACTIVITY #2

Step One—Internalizing Permissions: Review the list of Permissions you developed while learning Basic Technique #2—Asking for Permissions From Others. For each of those Permissions you received from others, practice giving them to yourself, using the following format:

Question: "Will I give myself Permission to ＿＿＿＿＿＿ ?"
Answer: "Yes, I can ＿＿＿＿＿＿ ."

Example: "Will I give myself Permission to *be more playful*?"
"Yes, I can *have fun and play.*"

Step Two—Deal With Your Resistance: Write each Self-Permission on the left side of a page; on the right side, write any thoughts or feelings that run counter to the Permission. Rewrite each resistance as a new Self-Permission on the left until no more resistance appears.

Examples:

Yes, I can have fun and play.	But other people know how and I don't.
I can have fun learning how to play.	
I can enjoy feeling silly.	I will feel silly.
I can be spontaneous and do exactly what I want to do.	But I won't know what to do.
I surely want to have more fun.	
I feel like really letting go. I want to run and play and be a child again.	
My ability to play and have fun is unlimited.	
I can now create infinite opportunities to play and have fun.	

_____
_____
_____
_____
_____
_____
_____
_____

Step Three—Acting on Your Permissions: The final step is acting upon a Self-Permission by doing something you previously would not have done. Go back to each Permission when you have dissolved the resistance and say or write the following:

    "Yes, I can _____

"What I am going to do with this Permission is _____.
_____
_____

"What I hope to get out of doing this is."

_____
_____
_____

Example: "Yes, I can *have fun and play.*
"What I am going to do with this Permission is *spend a half hour today watching children play in the park.*
"What I hope to get out of doing this is *more information about how to play and more Permission to play.*"

HOW OTHERS HAVE USED SELF-PERMISSIONS

Sid walked past a park every day to and from his parking lot and office. When he saw children playing, he sometimes felt sad. He thought to himself, "Gee, it's been a long time since I did that." He realized it was difficult for him to play because of his role as a businessman. His internalized ghost message was clear: "Playing is for children; when you grow up you have more important things to do."

Sid began to eat his lunch in the park on nice days instead of in the office cafeteria. One day, he really wanted to swing on the swings and slide down the sliding board. He said, "I can still play and have fun if I want to. I am going to swing and enjoy myself while I am here."

When Sid returned to the office, he seemed to have more life in him. Several people noticed how cheerful and happy he looked, and his secretary said, "Wow, you certainly must have had a good lunch today."

XIV WEAVING TOGETHER THE THREADS OF THE NEW YOU

OVERVIEW OF ADVANCED TECHNIQUES

By learning to use the three basic techniques, you have learned the skills necessary to begin changing your life. You no longer have to be a certain way if you don't want to be. Now you are ready to learn more advanced techniques to help you weave together the threads that enable you to live your life the way you want it to be.

UNDERSTANDING THE PROCESS OF REPROGRAMMING YOUR LIFE

If you had grown up in a simple, unchanging, agrarian society, your script probably could continue fairly constant without presenting many problems throughout your life. However, because you do live in a complex, rapidly changing, industrial society, it is likely that you will be forced to rewrite parts of your life script many times. This reprogramming process can be an exciting adventure, or it can be a horrible nightmare. The difference rests mainly in having the skills and information, or the tools, to cope with change. The skills and information have been developed, but up to now it has been difficult for most people to gain access to them and to learn them. None of the major institutions usually charged with teaching people what they need to get along in this world have focused on teaching people how to cope with change. Our schools, where this skill could be taught to most young people, have not seen this as their major responsibility. Some attention is paid to the personal and psychological effects of change, but skill in coping with change is not emphasized. By and large, established churches also have ignored this aspect. The home remains probably the only place where the effects of change are taught—and mostly by negative examples because the family is being destroyed by change and lack of awareness and skills to cope with it. Those professions that know the most about change and its effects—namely psychology and psychiatry—seemingly are not taking leadership to remedy the problem. In fact, they seem to be contributing to the problem by actively resisting attempts to place the tools of change and growth in the hands of the general public.[1] It is almost as though there were a conspiracy of silence to keep people afraid and dependent while change marches on.

ILLUSIONS, CULTURAL MYTHS, ASSUMPTIONS, AND ROLE EXPECTATIONS

Most life scripts are based upon some illusions, cultural myths, assumptions, and role expectations. Earlier we described how these concepts tend to dull your awareness of options and help keep you in restricted life patterns. An illusion is something that appears one way and is actually another way. Two pervasive illusions are "I control what happens to other people" and "I can make them love me or not love me." These script illusions are rooted in early parent-child interactions. Developmentally, children have poor cause-and-effect thinking before the age of two. Children believe they can cause a parent to go away or to come to them. In the case of an overprotected child, the parent supports the illusion of control by denying his/her own needs to serve the whims of the child. The whole developmental issue to be resolved at around the age of two is "Can I control my environment?"

A healthy resolution involves learning that you do things for your reasons, and other people do things for their reasons. Therefore, you can't control what others decide to do and they can't control what you do. The decision is to learn ways to get needs and wants met without trying to control. If you did not solve that developmental problem at the appropriate age, and many people don't, you will recycle it in adult relationships. The following example may show you how control illusions get processed in relationships.

Harry tends to have unsatisfactory relationships with women because he still listens to old script messages that tell him he is unlovable. Therefore, he thinks he must trick someone into loving him. He meets and goes out with Doris and he begins to work overtime to make her like him. He is charming and witty, and takes her flowers. He takes her out to a fancy dinner. Doris is overjoyed to find a man who lavishes so much attention on her, and she sees him as different from other men and as a good catch. She wants to explore ways to deepen and enrich the relationship, while Harry, sensing her deepening commitment, begins to feel guilty for "making her love him." He feels trapped because he believes he must be as committed as Doris is in order to maintain control of the relationship. Harry then scares himself about the level of commitment and withdraws more and more from Doris, who is left wondering what she did to chase Harry away.

Both Harry and Doris are operating out of illusions of control. This sounds like a soap opera, but is all too real in the lives of many people who, unknowingly, are stuck recycling sex-role script messages.

The biggest part of reprogramming your life is learning how to avoid the illusions on which your original script is based. For most people, this is almost a life-long process. Let us begin with the notion of the illusion of control. You have read about its origins. Now you will have a chance to look at how much you use that illusion by taking the following inventory.

Place a check mark in the column that best describes how frequently you respond to situations using the illusion of control.

ILLUSION INVENTORY

Situation	Never	Sometimes	Usually	Always
1. Get angry at other people for causing you problems.				
2. Have a hard time shifting gears if things don't turn out as you planned.				
3. Like to do things following a set routine.				
4. Don't like to sit and do nothing unless your work is all done first.				
5. Like things neat and tidy.				
6. Don't like having people tell you what to do.				
7. Feel guilty if someone gets angry at you.				
8. Tend to put off doing things until the last minute.				
9. Feel hurt if other people don't want to do what you want to do.				
10. Hold secret grudges against people who you think are unkind.				
Column Scores				

Total Score _____

Scoring: For each question, place a 1, 2, 3, or 4 (1 = Never; 4 = Always) in the column where you marked your answer. Add the numbers in each column to get a total score. The degree to which you use the control illusion is rated below.

1–19 low to none
20–29 moderate
30+ high

Try a short experiment with yourself. Exhale gently and then wait for your next breath to begin by itself. Do it again. If you find you are getting anxious while waiting for your next breath, it is likely you are trying to control more than is necessary, even your own breathing. Later in this chapter is an activity to help you learn how to give up your control illusions.

SCRIPT MYTHS

Myths are taught beliefs that you and others in your culture have come to believe are "good," "true," or "right," without much basis in fact. Examples are "Big boys don't cry," "People should be fair," "I must be liked by everyone I meet." If you need to identify any other myths you have believed in the process of growing up, check back to the Common Script Myths chart in Chapter IX. Cultural myths are often what bolt down many of your script decisions, so loosening these bolts may help you to decide what parts of your script need changing.

ASSUMPTIONS AND ROLE EXPECTATIONS

Assumptions are thoughts or ideas you believe are true but never check out. When you "assume" something, you are likely to make an "ass" out of "u" and "me." [3] "I assumed you wanted to make love tonight." "I assumed you would remember my birthday." We use assumptions to try to manipulate and control others.

Make a list of common assumptions. Complete the following (do as many as you can):

"I tend to assume _____."

"I tend to assume _____."

_____

_____

Example: "I tend to assume *my wife will have dinner ready for me when I come home.*" "I tend to assume *people don't like me if they don't look me in the eye.*"

Role expectations are much like assumptions, in that people behave as if these prescribed behaviors are important although no one really knows why they exist.

Sex-role or job-role expectations are common. Complete the following sentences to identify your sex-role expectations and stereotypes:

Women are _____ .

Women are _____ .

Women are _____ .

etc . _____ .

Men are _____ .

Men are _____ .

Men are _____ .

etc. _____ .

In some scripts, these expectations can be important ghost messages that restrict your functioning as a person. It is important to examine your sex-role beliefs and expectations and decide which ones to keep and which ones to change. In Chapter XVII, you will find additional information on the effects of role expectations on parenting, teaching, managing, relating, etc.

ADVANCED TECHNIQUE #1: USING PERMISSIONS TO HELP REWRITE YOUR SCRIPT

Activity #1: Giving Up Control Illusions

Rationale: Giving up illusions that anchor your script can provide you with new information and Permissions that help you change your script.

Step One: Make a list of all the ways you try to

control yourself and others. Use the open-ended sentence "I try to control by _____."

Step Two: Now go back over your list and write down how you would behave or think differently if you no longer believed you had control of yourself or others. Example: "I would feel my feelings more." In some instances you won't have to do anything differently because the illusion was only in your thinking and not evident in your behavior.

Step Three: Examine your new thoughts and behaviors and determine what specific Permissions you want. Example: "It is good for me to experience my feelings." Identify any ghost messages that counter each Permission. Example: "Bad things happen to you when you let yourself feel your feelings."

Step Four: Design a strategy to strengthen the power of the Permission message and weaken the power of the ghost message. Example: "I will make a list of good things that will happen to me because I feel my feelings more."

Activity #2:
Demything Your Script

Rationale: The things you believed were true when you wrote parts of your script may not be true anymore. Reevaluating your beliefs to remove myths is an essential part of rewriting your script.

Step One: Write all the things you believed were true while you were growing up that you later learned were not true. Example: "Parents are perfect."

Step Two: Write all the things you wish you had known or believed while you were growing up. These are the things that you believe would have made a difference in how you saw yourself, others and the world. Example: "I am a lovable person."

Step Three: In the list in step two are some of the Permissions you likely still want and need. Look at your list and design a strategy for getting each of these Permissions. *"You deserve to get what you want and need."*

Activity #3: Dealing with Role Expectations

Rationale: We play many roles because of the cultural and family script messages to which we listen. These roles and expectations tend to lower awareness of options for solving problems and often encourage people to lead stereotyped, banal lives.

Step One: Write "I am _____" ten times. Each time, write down a role that you play to complete the sentence. Example, "I am a father," or "I am a son."

Step Two: After each of your ten roles, complete the following: "In order for me to be a good _____ , I must _____ ." Example: "In order for me to be a good *son*, I must be *successful.*"

Step Three: Rank order the ten roles from least important (10) to most important (1). Starting with the least important, cross out one at a time and write down what your life would be like without that role. Do this until you have eliminated all of the ten roles.

Step Four: Again write "I am _____" ten times, without using any of the previous roles. Example: "I am me."

Step Five: After each item of your second list of ten, write the following: "Because I choose to be _____ , I will _____ ." Example: "Because I choose to be *me,* I will *take time and energy to learn to know myself well.*" This statement then becomes the new Permission for you to change your roles and role expectations. Rewrite those parts of your script you want to change.

Activity #4: What's Important

Rationale: This programmed activity is designed to help you identify your most important values and beliefs. These can form the basis for rewriting a new script or may merely help you decide if you are satisfied with your script the way it is now.

Step One: Imagine you have just been told by your physician that you have six weeks to live. You have a disease which will permit you to function fairly much as you now do, but it is incurable. Imagine you have $20,000 in cash from a savings account available to you.

Step Two: Think about and write what you would do with your last six weeks. How would you spend your last six weeks of life? What would you do with $20,000?

Step Three: Look over what you have decided you would do. What does this tell you about what is important to you? How many of the things that are important to you are you already doing now? If you are not doing them, look at how you are using your old script messages to keep yourself from doing what you want to do. Make a list of things you would like to change about your script in order to enjoy what is important to you.

Step Four: Next to each part of your script that you want to change, write a Permission message that you want and need in order to make that change.

Activity #5: Permissions to Rewrite Your Script

Rationale: In this activity, think about specific behaviors or habits you want to change. Here you are learning how to redesign and engineer your script.

Step One: Think of a behavior or habit you want to change. Write the following: "I would like to _____

_____."

Example: "I would like to *quit smoking.*"

Step Two: Write "I won't _____

_____."

Example: "I won't *quit smoking.*" Write this over and over on a sheet of paper and say it to yourself over and over until you are really tired of writing and hearing it (this is really important).

Step Three: Now, close your eyes and fantasize what you will be like in five, ten, fifteen years if you continue this unwanted behavior (smoking). Fully realize all the implications of this behavior on your life pattern. Write down any thoughts or impressions.

Step Four: Now, write "I will _____

_____."

Example: "I will *quit smoking.*" Write and say this over and over until you know you really mean it.

Step Five: Now, close your eyes and fantasize how you will be, feel, act, and behave in a year, five, ten, fifteen years having given up this unwanted behavior.

Step Six: Write, "I am sad to give up this behavior because _____

_____."

and write, "I am happy to give up this behavior because _____."
Write these sentences as many times as you need to understand your feelings.

Step Seven: Write any Permissions you want and need to change this behavior or habit. Design a strategy for giving yourself and/or getting from others these Permissions: *"You are in charge, so*

you can change anything that no longer fits your new script."

HOW OTHERS HAVE USED PERMISSIONS TO REWRITE THEIR SCRIPTS

George is a rather shy, gentle man, soft-spoken, respectful, and thoughtful of others. He spends considerable time and energy trying to control things carefully so he can avoid being vulnerable and also avoid situations in which he feels scared. Occasionally, when he is having a more difficult time controlling things, he gets scared and takes a couple of drinks to bolster his courage. If drinking doesn't bring immediate relief, he may drink more so that he finds "fault" with the actions of persons close to him and abuses them with an angry verbal barrage. Afterward, he remembers little of what he said, is back in control, and feels safe.

Because it was not acceptable for George to feel and express anger as a child, he learned to try to control this feeling. George finally decided to start therapy to deal with this problem, and it soon became apparent that George had not forgiven his parents and was hanging on to some anger toward them. With the help of considerable support and Permissions, George talked to his parents and had the first real conversation with them that he had ever had. He also realized that he no longer wanted to use his anger to try to control others. He agreed to stop using alcohol to drown out his anger and fright, and instead, to use new ways to express them. He began to write out Permissions on cards and carry them with him as reminders. *"I can stay in touch with my feelings and ask for what I want from others if I am scared or angry."*

George has not had one of his fits of temper in over six months. He is well on his way to rewriting that part of his script which read, "George is in control of everything, including his feelings." George's script now reads, "George is a gentle, feeling man who lets you know how he is feeling, even when he is angry."

XV USING PERMISSIONS TO CHANGE YOUR LIFE'S DECISIONS

MAN, UNLIKE THE ANIMALS,
HAS NEVER LEARNED THAT
THE SOLE PURPOSE OF LIFE
IS TO ENJOY IT.
NOTE-BOOKS, SAMUEL BUTLER

UNDERSTANDING YOUR NEED FOR REDECISIONS

Only in the past decade has the study of human behavior focused on the normal course of development, and on the role of parent figures in this normal growth and development. While information is now more readily available to professionals, the average person has not been affected by this information. Until every parent is trained to use these concepts and skills, children probably will continue to grow up making restrictive and sometimes debilitating decisions about important areas of their lives.

Though it would have been better for you to have been equipped with the tools to handle your life effectively in the first place rather than try to undo the harm that has been done, there is still much reason to hope. First, childhood decisions were just that, *decisions*. They were made consciously, even though the awareness of the original decision may be buried; and they can be consciously redecided again by acquiring additional information and skills. Second, there is good information now available to you in making redecisions. Third, the necessary skills can be rather easily taught to you. Fourth, change is becoming far more acceptable in our society, so more and more people are getting Permission from their environment to change restrictive childhood script decisions. Fifth, we now know that any unresolved developmental issues recycle naturally anyway, so access to childhood decisions is easier than once thought. Sixth, because of rapid social change, scripts based upon childhood decisions are "running out" earlier in life. Finally, Permission Theory holds as one of its basic premises that you are capable of identifying and understanding how your childhood decisions are affecting your life. Freudian and other dynamic theories do not give people enough credit; they maintain that much of your childhood remains a lost mystery which you are not capable of understanding. Permission Theory differs completely from that point of view. For all of these reasons, you do not have to stay trapped in a restrictive life with few options. *You can regain the natural wholeness with which you were born.*

IDENTIFYING CHILDHOOD DECISIONS

If your childhood seems like a faint memory, about all you need to do is open your mouth to realize you never left it. In one sense, you spend all your life trying to grow up; and in another sense, you spend the same time trying to restore the wholeness of your being—the wholeness that was yours at your birth.[1] No matter which way you are going, you will meet your childhood decisions on the way. Childhood script decisions are ways you order your world, and if these decisions are not changed, they continue to influence every breath you take.[2]

In chapters VII and VIII, you learned how you made your original script decisions and how to identify the presence of the decisions in your present behavior. A basic principle of Permission Theory is that one of your basic needs is to restore your natural wholeness. You are constantly creating situations in which you have opportunities to remove the blocks to that wholeness. Your childhood script decisions do function as major blocks to wholeness. Because you fail to see this process for what it is, you end up strengthening the decision rather than making a redecision. Armed with a new awareness, you can add the other ingredients essential for redecisions: permissions and specific skills.

Making a redecision is very much like pulling out one block at the base of a tower of blocks; the tower comes tumbling down and has to be rebuilt. It takes courage to pull out that block, and it takes information and skills to rebuild the tower with a new foundation. Permissions are useful in both parts of the process. It *is* a process, and once it is learned, the process can be applied over and over again. Your first redecision will be your most difficult one. There is an almost irreversible first step, and once it is taken there is no turning back. It is like learning to ski. The first time you turn the skis downhill and start moving, you know you can't go back. You don't know what will happen next and somehow time stands still for a moment. Then you are totally engulfed in the process of skiing. The next time there will still be a fear, though not as much, for you have been down that hill before. Just as you would not start skiing on an experts' slope, you would not begin learning the redecision process with your most difficult problem.

Where do you start? Identification of the nature and degree of your childhood decision is the best place to start. In addition to those activities presented earlier in the book, another aid to identification will be presented later in this chapter.

RECYCLING CHILDHOOD DECISIONS

As mentioned above, you are constantly recycling the script decisions you are ready to change. Understanding how to identify the recycling process is also part of identifying your decisions in action. Development is continuous, there are always new tasks to be learned, and any task not learned in its proper time and place is dragged along as excess baggage. Any time you are learning a new developmental task, you are likely to stumble over a leftover one, too.[3]

You will know that you have "leftover" tasks when:

—Your feelings seem more intense than a situation calls for.

—You don't seem to be able to think of very many options for solving a problem.

—You place your spouse or friends in a parent role in order to get them to be responsible for you (blaming someone else for your problems).

—You attempt to relive your past through your children's experiences (push them to do what you didn't do).

—You start doing things you didn't get to do at an earlier age/stage of development (the forty-year-old woman who suddenly starts buying teenage styles of clothing, or the quiet accountant who suddenly starts playing harmless practical jokes).

If you can recognize and separate the here-and-now aspects of a problem and the past aspects being recycled, you are well on the way to making a redecision. For example, you may think and solve problems quite effectively and then suddenly be faced with a situation where you stop thinking. Perhaps the common element is an authority figure putting some pressure on you to think. This may have taken you back to a situation where as a child you were unable to please a parent or teacher in a similar situation. In the original situation you may have perceived that you had no options. As a result you may have immobilized yourself in the present situation and may not be able to see even obvious options. Once you learn to recognize and separate the two situations you will be able to overcome the problem.

An important way to separate the present and past aspects of a problem is to learn to check out the reality of a present situation. Since most of your childhood decisions were made in situations where you believed your safety or survival depended on making that decision, you reexperience some safety- or survival-level thoughts and feelings. If you check to see if the present problem involves survival, safety, or comfort issues, you can begin to separate the present from the past. Almost all present problems involve comfort/discomfort issues and not safety or survival. The safety or survival feelings, then, are attached to the past part of the problem and usually involve the childhood decision. The following example illustrates this process even more clearly.

Joan was an unplanned and unwanted menopausal baby. Her mother had wanted to resume studying art after her children were grown, and she resented having to delay her studies when Joan arrived. She unconsciously pushed Joan to grow up faster than Joan needed or wanted. She also suffered over the responsibilities of child rearing, and in Joan's presence she freely and frequently spoke about her daughter as a burden.

Joan was rewarded for being a good girl. She decided early that she had to please her parents and take care of them by not causing them any trouble. Thus, she could get strokes for doing what they wanted. As a result she received mostly "doing" strokes (for doing what her parents wanted) rather than "being" strokes (unconditional strokes such as "you are a fine person").

In school, Joan tried to please her teachers to obtain performance strokes, even though she knew somehow they were not what she wanted. She worked hard to be popular and was always on a diet. When she was scared that she was not very important, she would drive herself harder and do more of what she thought others wanted so they would like her. She would often have anxiety attacks as she took on more and more responsibility. Some mornings she would awaken curled up like a baby, sucking her thumb. She began biting her fingernails and picking at her cuticles until they bled.

At the age of nineteen, after trying business school for a year and not liking it, Joan decided to get married. She now devoted herself completely to pleasing her husband to get her performance strokes and, she hoped, an unconditional one now and then. However, she chose a man who, much like her father, was too busy with a career to pay much attention to her. He gave her some praise for her cooking, but not much other attention. In fact, her husband picked at her much of the time, as her mother had. He often found fault with things that she did and said. When they entertained Pete's co-workers, Joan wanted to make a good impression so she would be rewarded with some strokes. She would talk about anything just to continue talking, and Pete would become angry as he sensed his guest's discomfort with Joan's performance. She would drink heavily and talk loudly. After their guests left, Pete would lecture her about her behavior. Remorseful, she would promise never to do it again. Joan could continue with her early decision and burn out, ending up angry, lonely, and possibly dying a slow death.

First-Degree Redecision: Joan decided she wanted to change what she was doing. First, she returned to school in search of a career. She met other women who were also interested in changing. They eventually formed a consciousness-raising group in which Joan began to get feedback and to get a clear idea about what she really wanted. She began to like herself for who she was and not for what she did. She began to ask for unconditional strokes more, because of the Permissions she received from her CR group. She learned to give herself Permissions and to let the strokes really soak in. She also took a Transcendental Meditation course and gave herself Permission to practice it several times a day. She redecided that she was important and fine as she was. She decided not to perform to get the strokes of others but to feel good about herself.

UNDERSTANDING THE PROCESS OF REDECISIONS [4]

Like other techniques you have learned, there is a process to learn with redecisions. The redecision process has at least three distinct stages. They can take five minutes or many months to complete. The pace is your choice. The first stage involves a clear decision to redecide. The techniques you learned in the previous chapters are often part of making that decision. Learning to forgive your parents is very important in redecisions because your original decision was to let them or make them take responsibility for that part of your life. Learning to get the Permissions you want and need strengthens your decision and weakens the effects of the ghost messages related to the childhood decision. The Permission process is strengthened even more by your learning the internal power of giving Permissions to yourself and no longer listening to your now weakened ghost messages.

The second stage involves moving to an impasse where turning back seems impossible and going ahead too scary. You may experience the redecision at this stage as involving irreconcilable opposites (e.g., "How can I decide to be really close when I am so afraid I can't enjoy it anyway?"). You may get stuck here, retreat from the redecision, move back to the first stage to build more support or move through the impasse to stage three.

Stage three, on the other side of the impasse, involves rebuilding a structure on a new foundation. Many things which were seen only one way before are now understood in a new and often much deeper way.

ADVANCED TECHNIQUE #2: USING PERMISSIONS TO MAKE REDECISIONS

Activity #1: Identifying Developmental Decisions

Rationale: Numerous direct and indirect messages influenced your childhood decisions. This activity may help you do some detective work on yourself to identify, at each stage of development, the messages that may have led to your childhood decisions.

Step One: Imagine you are one of your parents (or a parent figure whose messages may have influenced you) telling someone else about you when you were various ages (e.g., Father, about birth: "I am really happy it's a boy"). Choose the parent you think had the most influence on you at that age. Also, use both parents when appropriate. Think about what your parents might have said to other people (friends, relatives, etc.) about you.

Step Two: For each of the ages listed below, write as many messages as you can imagine each or both parents might have given others about you. Use your imagination and play hunches. Guess if you don't know.

When you were born _____
_____
_____

Up to six months _____
_____
_____

Six to eighteen months _____
_____
_____

Eighteen months to three years _____
_____
_____

Three to six years _____
_____
_____

Six to twelve years _____
_____
_____

Twelve to eighteen years _____
_____
_____

Now _____
_____

Step Three: Now, go back over your list and place a check mark next to those messages that still influence you today. Then make a list of the ways you are still influenced by those messages.

Step Four: Using the list of the eleven most common childhood decisions, identify which decisions you made as a result of being influenced by these messages. Make a list of the decisions you think you made, the age when you think you made each decision, and what specific incidents you can remember being associated with each decision.

_____
_____
_____
_____
_____

Step Five: For each of the childhood decisions, identify a redecision you might make now. What positive effects would making that redecision have on your life? What negative effects, if any, do you see?

Step Six: If you were willing to make a redecision, what new messages (Permissions) would you want and need to replace the messages associated with the old decision? Make a list of as many new messages as you can.

_____
_____
_____
_____
_____

Step Seven: For each redecision area, fill out a Permission Chart similar to the one shown in Chapter IX. Identify the specific Permissions you are aware of wanting and needing from others and your environment. Refer back to Chapter IX for more information.

Permission Chart for _____ Redecision

	Verbal	Nonverbal
Direct Permissions		
Indirect Permissions		

Example:

Permission Chart for *I Won't Think*
Redecision

	Verbal	Nonverbal
Direct Permissions	"It is fine for *you* to think and take care of yourself."	Doing crossword puzzles.
Indirect Permissions	Observing someone receiving above Direct Permission	Learning to play a musical instrument

Activity #2: Deciding to Redecide

Rationale: Now that you have information about your childhood decisions and their effects, you can begin the redecision process. If you have identified several possible redecisions, start with the one that is most clear to you.

Step One: Using the redecision structure presented in Chapter IX, fill in with the redecision you want to make.

Redecision: _____
Redecision structure:
Since I, _____,
                  (your name)
decided that_____
                 (original decision)
I,_____ will now redecide that
  (your name)
_____.
            (new decision)
What I will get out of this is_____

_____,
         (positive consequence)
and I,_____, will _____
    (your name)

_____
         (Self-Permission)

Example:
Redecision: *To be real, to be important.*
Redecision structure:
"Since I, _____, decided that *I was not worthwhile*, I, _____, will now redecide *that I am worthwhile*. What I will get out of this is *to feel good about myself*, and I, _____, *will feel good about myself*."

Step Two: Write the Self-Permission you used in the Redecision Structure on the left side of the sheet of paper, and on the right side write the old script messages to which you are still listening that help you resist making the redecision. Take each old script message and rewrite it on the left as a Self-Permission.

Example:

"I, Barry Weinhold, feel good about myself."	"Who do you think you are?"
"I, Barry Weinhold, am a lovable and capable person."	"You'll never amount to anything."
"I, Gail Andresen, am successful at whatever I decide to do."	

Activity #3: Getting Through the Impasse

Rationale: Some people experience a stuck feeling in the middle of making a redecision. People have described it as a pause before taking the plunge. The experience can be momentary or long. If it happens to you, then use the following activity to assist you in getting through the impasse.

Step One: Write, "I have gotten myself stuck because _____." Write this sentence as many different ways as you can to get a full awareness of what information you are using to get yourself stuck.

Step Two: Take your "stuckness" one step further and write, "How I will keep myself stuck is

_____

_____."
         (negative payoff)

Write that as many times as you can fill in the blanks with new responses.

Step Three: Now really get into being stuck. Write, "I won't decide to _____." Write this over and over on a sheet of paper and say it over and over to yourself or others until you are really tired of writing and hearing it. This is important for getting yourself unstuck.

Step Four: Now, close your eyes and fantasize what you will be like in five, ten, fifteen years if you continue operating on your childhood decision. Realize the full implications of not making this redecision. Write any thoughts or feelings you are having.

Step Five: Now try the other side of the impasse. Write, "How I will get myself unstuck is _____." Identify as many ways as you can use to get unstuck.

Step Six: Write, "I will redecide to _____." Write this over and over until you are sure you really mean it.

Step Seven: Now, close your eyes and begin to fantasize how your life will be different after you have redecided. Project your fantasy ahead a year, five, ten, fifteen years. Write out your thoughts and feelings.

Step Eight: Check out your feelings one more time. Write, "I am sad about changing my childhood decision because _____." Write, "I am happy about making this redecision because _____." Write those sentences as many times as you need to get clear of your feelings.

Activity #4: Implementing Your Redecision

Rationale: After making the redecision, you may find it takes some time to reorder your thinking and behavior. You are in transition, and you may need some ways of learning to understand and accept being in transition. Chapter X contains further information on being in transition.

Step One: Write and complete the three following sentences:

"I am in transition from _____.",

"I am in transition and _____."

"I am in transition toward _____."

Step Two: Now, examine how much you have invested in defining yourself as being in transition from, just being in transition, or being in transition toward some goal. Assign a percentage to each statement with the three percentages equaling one hundred percent. (*"You can trust your perceptions of yourself."*)

Step Three: Practice using transition Permissions, both with yourself and in describing yourself to others. Complete the following transition Permissions and use them with the redecision you made.

"I used to _____
                    (old behavior)
but now I don't do that as much anymore. I am learning to _____
                    (new behavior)
and now I'm able to do that more often. Even

though I have redecided _____,

I still occasionally do _____.
                    (old behavior)

I now do _____
                    (new behavior)

and hardly ever do _____
                    (old behavior)

anymore."

"I Can Take My Time and Learn to _____."

"I Don't Have to Be Perfect to Feel Good About My New Decision."

REDECISIONS OTHERS HAVE MADE

Katherine was the daughter of Irish Catholic parents. Her father was an alcoholic and was rarely at home; her mother was the strong one in the family. With six children and a father who continually lost jobs, the family often went cold and hungry. Kate learned early, at a basic survival level, that her needs didn't count. Much of this programming was supported by her church. She learned that she would probably have to suffer. Her only salvation was to deny her needs and to give to others. When she graduated from high school, she entered nurses' training and became a registered nurse. After school, she entered the Peace Corps and served in Latin America for two years.

When Kate returned to the U.S., she met and married a man who drank heavily and couldn't hold a job. She spent the next ten years having five children and trying to save her husband from himself. Her position was to make others happy and not to think about herself. She tried to make her husband happy sexually, even though he consistently abused her physically. She even blamed herself when he finally deserted her and their family.

Out of necessity, Kate returned to nursing. However, she didn't enjoy her work and resented always having to give so much of herself to her patients—just as she also devoted herself to her family. Kate became depressed and started taking sleeping pills at night and "uppers" in the morning.

First-Degree Redecision: Kate decided to take

an in-service class in TA and Nursing at the hospital where she worked. Here she learned about Rescuing and about her self-denial script. At one of the class sessions, she participated in an exercise in which she had to ask for what she wanted. Realizing that Kate was experiencing difficulty with the exercise, the instructor came to her and said, "Kate, you can put your own needs first and ask for what you want." Kate looked at Ms. Carson, her instructor, and said, "I really want to believe that. I am going to stop Rescuing others and start putting myself first."

XVI USING PERMISSIONS TO STAY CURRENT WITH YOURSELF

THEY MUST OFTEN CHANGE
WHO WOULD BE CONSTANT
IN HAPPINESS AND WISDOM.
—CONFUCIUS

UNDERSTANDING THE NEED FOR ONGOING CHANGE

You are living through a period of the greatest changes in recorded history. You are living in the middle of a revolution—a values revolution. No one agrees as to when it began, but almost everyone who is aware of the revolution knows of its effects. All major established values and beliefs have been challenged, and as never before, they are in a constant state of confusion and change. Values regarding sex roles, drugs, work, and leisure, and even the meaning of life itself, are all undergoing rapid change.[1] These swift changes are both scary and exciting.

Since most people's basic attitudes and values regarding these issues are formed by about the age of ten, they are part of your individual script ledger. When you change your values or beliefs in any of the above areas, the parts of your script connected to those values will also change. Scripts that used to last a lifetime are now "running out" by the age of thirty, forty, or even earlier.

Writer Gail Sheehy, in her book *Passages*, describes the predictable life crises that occur at various ages. Although Sheehy offers little about the causality of these crises, it appears from her descriptions that they are the result of obsolete scripts running out prematurely. She writes that ". . . a new vitality springs from within as we approach 30. Men and women alike speak of feeling narrow and restricted." Sheehy says people tend to blame others for causing these restrictions, "but what the restrictions boil down to are the outgrowth of career and personal choices of the twenties." The task, then, seems to be one of making new choices or rewriting your script. For most people, such a task creates a life crisis.[2]

Sheehy also identifies the decade from thirty-five to forty-five as "a time of both danger and op-portunity," a time during which we have a "chance to rework the narrow identity by which we defined ourselves in the first half of life."[3]

Although it is not central to her treatise, Sheehy highlights the Permission process as an important part of change and growth. She writes that when we discover we are in charge of ourselves, "we no longer have to ask permission because we are the providers of our own safety. We must learn to give ourselves permission."[4]

WHAT TO DO WHEN YOUR SCRIPT RUNS OUT

When a script runs out, it may mean that all your major goals have been attained, or that your hoped-for goals are no longer of any interest or appeal. No one is ever adequately prepared to deal with an obsolete script, and most of us may suffer during such a frightening experience. For some, it is like pulling the plug on a bathtub and seeing all the water slowly draining out. It seems as though there is nothing that can be done to prevent the emptiness.

You can temporarily plug the drain, but you can't do much else to remedy the situation. Some people frantically try to add more water and try even harder to maintain their script. Others may seek out someone to tell about their plight in hopes that another person may be able to plug the drain. Still others become depressed and even incapacitated because they do not know how to cope with the situation.

Nervous breakdowns and so-called mental illnesses are common in the age bracket of thirty to sixty, and may occur when major aspects of a script run out or when a person incapacitates himself/herself. Some people become obsessed with fears of going crazy, growing old, dying, or being helpless and powerless. They may quit their jobs, leave their families, wander aimlessly in search of some way to avoid the inevitable. Some people may find temporary ways to avoid the inevitable, but in the final analysis there is no way to run away from yourself. The information and skills in this book alone can give you the tools to deal with your life when your script runs out.

SCRIPTS DIE A SLOW DEATH

Scripts usually do not run out all at once. You do get many early warning signals, and you must be able and willing to pay attention to them. Sometimes, however, a traumatic event, such as a debilitating illness or the death of a loved one can trigger the awareness that your script is running out. This is particularly true of people who have failed to heed the early warning signals. Common early warning signals are as follows:

—You see life passing you by, and you are not moving with it.

—You find that very few things you are doing are the things you really enjoy.

—You become bored with your job.

—You experience moments of sadness for no apparent reason.

—You think about the past more often.

—You think your future seems bleak or scary.

—You feel trapped by your circumstances and feel helpless to change them.

—You have lost interest in things you once considered fascinating.

—You feel the best part of your life is over.

—You need more artificial stimulants, such as drugs and alcohol, to function.

—You seem to be waiting for things to happen *to* you, rather than making things happen *for* you.

If you identify with any of the above situations, it is likely that parts of your script are indeed running out. This does not mean you should panic or scare yourself. We suggest you use the activities later in this chapter to cope effectively with any fear or anxiety you may be experiencing.

FIRST THINGS FIRST

If you are aware that your script is running out, there are several immediate things you may begin doing.

1. Begin to identify the things that are most important in your life.

2. Keep functioning! Some people let their fears immobilize them. Make yourself lists of things to do or structure your time with friends and don't lose your momentum.

3. Continue to nurture and take good care of yourself. Establish regular meal and sleep habits.

4. Do something fun every day.

5. Explore available community resources (e.g., employment or career counseling).

6. Take a vacation.

7. Get plenty of Permissions and support from others. Ask for the specific Permissions you want and need.

8. Talk to other people who have been successful at rewriting their scripts. Find out how they have changed.

9. Think of things you enjoy doing and give yourself Permission to do them.

10. In addition to the other steps listed, you may want to seek therapy to help you write a new script.

All of these can be beneficial if you are losing momentum. Learn to keep generating new options for yourself! The activities later in this chapter may help you practice this skill.

DEVELOPING INTERNAL AWARENESS

When everything around you is in a constant state of change, it is harder to rely upon external standards or trends. Your best information comes from your own internal processes, with which you can identify and stay current. Like most people, you were probably taught to look outside of yourself for stability, and you will have to learn to refocus upon your inner self. You may need to get to know yourself better and begin to sort out what is important and lasting in your life so that stability can evolve naturally. Since many people have been taught to distrust their own perceptions, thoughts, beliefs, and values, a refocusing process may be difficult at first.

One way to learn to tune in to your internal processes is to develop the skill of *thought watching*. Devote several minutes each day to focusing inward, paying attention to your thoughts. Don't evaluate or try to change your thoughts; just follow them. See where they are going. This appears to be a simple exercise, but some people report having considerable difficulty following their thoughts. Other meditative techniques can extend this process to the point of going beyond thoughts to a relaxed state of mind where no thinking occurs.

BEHAVING AS IF

One of the most difficult things you may ever do is exist in a constant state of change. Being in transition often means that old ways no longer fit and new ways are not yet comfortable and integrated. The major requirement of this transition period is trust or faith in the viability of new decisions and behaviors. This may be regarded *as if* you *know* a new decision or behavior will be validated. Learning how to act *as if* will help you over some rough spots when you feel you are between a rock and a hard place.

FOR THE RECORD

One of the most effective means many people use for keeping current with themselves is a daily journal or diary. A journal can help you make contact with your inner resources and reconnect you with your own life processes. Particularly when change is occurring all around you, a record of your thoughts, feelings, fantasies, and dreams, over time, can provide you with a stability and direction.[5]

Later in this chapter is an activity to help you begin learning the journal-keeping skill. The best way to learn journal keeping is to experiment with it and develop the method that fits you best. Below are some general guidelines to help you get started.

1. Do your journal at the same time each day. Choose a time, perhaps before going to sleep at night, to make an entry.

2. Make your entries brief and descriptive. After you have made short entries, elaborate on any you wanted to explore further.

3. In deciding what entries to make, go back over your day and ask yourself some of the following questions: How were you feeling when you went to bed? Got up in the morning? What kind of relationships did you experience during your day? What feelings do you recall during your day? and What changes in feelings did you experience during the day?

ADVANCED TECHNIQUE #3: USING PERMISSIONS TO STAY CURRENT WITH YOURSELF [6]

Activity #1: Taking Charge, Using Permissions

Rationale: As mentioned in Chapter I, we have over 50,000 thoughts each day, some positive and creative, and some negative and destructive. You can learn to take charge of whichever thoughts,

positive or negative, are predominant in your daily life. The more you use your positive thoughts as part of a creative process, the more positive growth and change you will bring into your life. Conversely, the more you use your negative thoughts as part of a destructive process, the more you will suffer and the more your life will remain painfully unchanging.

Step One: One way to teach yourself to use the power of your thoughts is to make Permission lists for yourself. Make a list of the ten most important Permissions you want and need for change and growth.

_____

_____

_____

_____

_____

_____

_____

_____

_____

_____

Step Two: Take each Permission and write a full page about that Permission. Elaborate on it. Explore your feelings again. Keep writing until you have filled a whole page with one Permission.

_____

_____

_____

_____

_____

_____

_____

_____

_____

_____

_____

_____

_____

_____

Step Three: To reinforce positive Permissions, start by recording all your Permissions on a cassette recorder and then listen to the tape repeatedly during the day. Listen to it while you are shaving, showering, eating, driving to work, making dinner, or any time you need to refocus your thoughts on positive things.

Activity #2: Goal Setting Using Permissions [7]

Rationale: One of the most important activities for you when your script begins to run out is to provide many options for yourself. People who are able to generate options seem to find new and exciting ways to change their scripts. The following activity is designed to produce a maximum number of choices.

Step One: Buy several packs of three-by-five index cards so you have a total of 300 cards.

Step Two: Putting one on each card, write one hundred things you would like to do. Include everything you have always wanted to do but were afraid to try.

Step Three: Again, with one item per card, write one hundred personality traits or talents you would like to have.

Step Four: With the remaining cards, list one hundred possessions you would like to have. List all material and nonmaterial things you have always dreamed of owning.

Step Five: Now you have three hundred options from which to choose. Select one of the three hundred cards that looks interesting to you and concentrate on what you wrote.

Step Six: Write a whole page about this goal and the Permissions you would need and want to reach this goal.

Step Seven: Design a strategy for reaching your goal (*You Deserve to Get What You Want and Need*).

_____

_____

_____

_____

Activity #3: Recovering Lost Goals and Aspirations[8]

Rationale: During the time when you were forming your original life plan (usually eight to sixteen years of age), you had many dreams and visions of what you wanted to accomplish during your lifetime. Many of these were discarded or forgotten as you narrowed your options. These dreams usually contain a combination of self-striving aspects (e.g., being successful or rich) and altruistic aspirations (e.g., serving others, doing something worthwhile). When your script begins to run out or change, you can recover these former goals and aspirations to determine if they could again become options to replace some part of your script that has run out. The following activity is designed to assist you in determining if certain old and discarded goals and aspirations could become a part of your new life plan.

Step One: Think back to your childhood and adolescence and make a list of the things you most wanted to do and be.

_____

_____

_____

_____

_____

_____

_____

_____

_____

_____

Step Two: Write your answers to the following questions about each goal listed in Step One:

A. How do you feel as you think about this rediscovered goal? What does it mean to you now?

B. How would your life be different now if you had achieved that goal?

C. How is that goal similar and/or different from the one(s) you chose to pursue instead?

D. What obstacles would you want or need to overcome if you decided to pursue this goal now?

Goal #1
A. _____
B. _____
C. _____
D. _____

Goal #2
A. _____
B. _____
C. _____
D. _____

Goal #3
A. _____
B. _____
C. _____
D. _____

Goal #4
A. _____
B. _____
C. _____
D. _____
Goal #5
A. _____
B. _____
C. _____
D. _____
Goal #6
A. _____
B. _____
C. _____
D. _____
Goal #7
A. _____
B. _____
C. _____
D. _____
Goal #8
A. _____
B. _____
C. _____
D. _____
Goal #9
A. _____
B. _____
C. _____
D. _____
Goal #10
A. _____
B. _____
C. _____
D. _____

Step Three: Choose the goals and aspirations you now wish to pursue and design a strategy to begin integrating them into your script. Use the following suggested format for recovering your lost goals:

A. The lost goal I am going to work on now is

_____ .

B. This goal is now important to me because

_____ .

C. My plans to reach this goal include:
1. Immediate plans _____

_____

2. Intermediate plans _____

_____

3. Long-range plans _____

_____

D. The Permissions I am going to want and need to reach this goal are: _____

_____ .

E. What I am going to do to get these Permissions is: _____

_____ .

F. I will give myself _____ (months/years) to work on this goal or aspiration.

Example:

A. The lost goal I am going to work on now is *being involved with young people as a coach or group leader.*

B. This goal is now important to me because *I enjoy working with young people in this way; I will get a great deal of satisfaction from this activity; I've always wanted to help others and haven't taken the time to do it.*

C. My plans to reach this goal include:

1. Immediate plans: *Calling the Park and Recreation Department to apply for a coaching job*

2. Intermediate plans: *Attending a coaching clinic to get more skills; reading more about coaching, talking with successful coaches*

3. Long-range plans: *Setting up recreational programs for kids, recruiting and training new coaches, and being a leader of leaders*

D. The Permissions I am going to want and need to reach this goal are *You can do something you always wanted to do. You are good at working with young people, and with practice you will get even better. You can set goals for yourself and work to achieve them.*

E. What I am going to do to get these Permissions is *Ask my friends for them, ask my spouse for support in reaching this goal, give myself Permission, and talk to other coaches about what they get out of coaching.*

A. _____

_____

B. _____

_____

C. 1._____

_____

2._____

_____

3._____

_____

D. _____

_____

E. _____

_____

F. I will give myself *two years* to work on this goal or aspiration.

Activity #4: Use a Period Journal to Stay Current With Yourself [9]

Rationale: All of us go through various periods or stages in our lives. This activity is designed to help you identify the current period of your life. Once you have identified the time of your life, you can stay current with your own life processes.

Step One: Close your eyes, relax, and focus inwardly for a while. Think about and answer this question for yourself: "Where am I in my life?" Let the answers to that question take shape by themselves; just watch your thoughts without judgments or evaluation. After you have followed your thoughts for several minutes, open your eyes and write anything you want about where you are in your life.

Step Two: With your eyes open, write as many statements as you can to complete the following open-ended sentence. "This period of my life is a time when I _____

_____."

Complete this sentence as many times and in as many different ways as possible.

_____

_____

_____

_____

_____

_____

_____

_____

Step Three: Now summarize in a few words what this time of your life means to you.

_____

_____

Step Four: Now begin to define the boundaries of this period of your life. When did this period begin? What events mark its beginning? Write down the significant facts relating to the beginning of this period.

_____

_____

_____

_____

_____

_____

_____

_____

Step Five: Imagine when this period will end and how it will end. What events will be part of the ending? Imagine you are at the end of this period of your life, looking backward. What do you see? How do you feel? What, if anything, would you do differently? Record the significant thoughts, feelings, and ideas you have about the end of this time of your life.

_____

_____

_____

_____

_____

_____

_____

HOW WE KEEP CURRENT WITH OURSELVES

Gail: How do you keep current with yourself?

Barry: First, I'm aware of my own internal processes. There does seem to be a pattern to the major changes I have made, say over the last ten to fifteen

113

years. Usually they have been made as the result of some crisis in my life.

G: What processes are you referring to? Give me an example.

B: I remember making a major life decision about thirteen years ago when I was in graduate school. The internal messages and processes that I had used to guide my life up until then could be summed up in the phrase: "I am a person to whom things happen." The decision I made was to be the kind of person who made things happen. This resulted in a number of new processes, such as taking initiative rather than waiting for something to happen.

G: How does being aware of those processes help you stay current with yourself?

B: Sometimes I lose track of those processes, so one important skill I have developed is occasionally stepping back and watching myself doing whatever I'm doing. Then I can decide, if I don't like what I'm doing, to do something else. This helps me realize that I can act and not merely react in life. I feel most alive when I am acting on the realization that I am in charge of making things happen for me.

How do you keep current with yourself?

G: I do something similar. I engage in a dialogue with myself. If I have made a decision to go ahead and be successful with something I am involved with, I will talk to the old ghost messages and hear them out. This helps me know how I may sabotage my own efforts. It also helps me know what Permissions to give myself or get from others to support my decision. Very often the Permissions I need are in the form of reassurances that nothing terrible is going to happen if I do this.

B: Another way I stay current with myself is by staying current with the other people I care for. I have fairly continuous long-term friendships with about six to eight people, and I stay fairly current with them. When I share with them what is happening with me, I also get a chance to watch myself to see what and how I share. Also, the feedback I get from them is helpful.

G: To be committed to that in your relationships is a very healthy way to stay current with yourself.

A way that I stay current with myself is by staying aware of the tensions in my muscles and the places in my body where I store feelings and unfinished business. If I seem to be storing up tension in my muscles, I take a look at what is going on with my day and think about what I need to do to release the tension.

B: Another method that I occasionally use to stay in touch with myself is through encounters with people whom I haven't seen for a while. I am always interested in knowing what changes they see in me since we last met. This has been helpful for me to validate the changes I've made.

G: Getting feedback can be scary for some people. Permissions can help some people accept feedback about how people see them changing.

B: At one time in my life when a friend would say, "Boy, you have changed," I would get scared. I wondered whether he thought the changes were good or bad. Now my instant response is "Thank you," even before I know what he means.

G: You must be feeling much better about yourself.

B: Yes, I am. I accept the fact that the changes I am making are for the better. When I look back at the changes I've made, they have always turned out to be positive, even though at the time it didn't seem as if they would.

G: One of the Permissions I would like our readers to share is that we have changed, are changing, and will continue to change our scripts. We refuse to stop growing and changing, because it is an exciting adventure.

B: I have come to believe that self-improvement isn't the most important goal in life; it is the only goal.

SECTION THREE

APPLICATION OF PERMISSION THEORY TO SPECIFIC ROLE-GROUPS

XVII FILLING THE HOLES IN ROLES

I CANNOT GIVE YOU THE
FORMULA FOR SUCCESS,
BUT I CAN GIVE YOU THE
FORMULA FOR
FAILURE—WHICH IS TRY TO
PLEASE EVERYBODY.
—HERBERT BAYARD SWOPE

How many of these statements do you believe are true?

—Parents should be consistent in setting rules and disciplining children.

—Teachers should not have favorite students.

—It is not desirable for bosses to express feelings in front of subordinates.

—The best relationships are those in which one's partner anticipates one's wants and needs before one has to ask.

—Children need to be protected from the evils of the real world.

All of the above statements are based upon social myths created to fit groups of people into roles. Have you ever noticed that people who belong to certain role groups sometimes share many common script myths?

For instance, many parents think their children should be seen and not heard, and many couples think expressing affection in public is undesirable.

The role groups we have selected for discussion are *parents, children, teachers, bosses,* and *couples.* It is common for many people who belong to role groups to think, "This is the only way to be," which means they are resigned to behaving in certain specified patterns and do not allow themselves to be aware of other options or alternatives. If the above conformance to the role is true, then how does change take place? Roles change because people decide to change. Permission to change is infectious when passed on to others and spreads like the common cold, only it is much more desirable.

PARENT TRAP

Common Myth of Parents	Myth-Breaker Permission
I'm responsible for how my children turn out (I take the blame or credit).	My children are ultimately responsible for how they turn out. I don't control them, and I can't or won't take credit for their successes or blame for their failures.

PERMISSION FOR PARENTS TO GIVE UP CONTROL

In evaluating your need to have control over your children, you can give yourself Permission to redecide, and allow your children to have control of their lives. As they grow older, they will need to decide to take responsibility for themselves anyway.

Brenda was fourteen and needed to experience her independence without totally moving out of her parents' home. She wanted to go places with her friends without having to share every detail with her mother. However, Brenda's mother would pounce on her the minute she entered the house. "Where did you go? Who were you with? What did you do? Brenda's mother wanted to maintain control of her, and Brenda resented her mother's cross-examination.

One day a female friend was visiting Brenda's mother when Brenda arrived home an hour late. Brenda's mother, as usual, interrogated her in the visitor's presence. Brenda, in frustration, raced outside yelling, "You don't trust me at all . . . I hate you!"

The friend confronted Brenda's mother, saying, "Brenda's old enough to be responsible. You can trust her. You can't control her, so you might as well stop demanding that she tell you all. She will tell you what she wants to and no more."

Brenda's mother thought about this comment for several days and then decided she was being unfair to her daughter. She stopped interrogating her daughter after this incident.

DILEMMAS OF CHILDHOOD

Common Myth of Children	*Myth-Breaker Permission*
It is essential that I follow the crowd so that I may be liked and accepted.	I can be unique and follow my own path. I can accept myself as I am and others can accept me for who I am.

PERMISSION FOR CHILDREN TO BE UNIQUE

By deciding to be the unique person you really are, you are giving yourself a Permission which will be long-lasting. Basically, this boils down to sticking up for your rights and getting from life what you want.

Manuel associated with a gang of tough guys, and he followed and obeyed the rules of the group. He had an inner conflict, but he did not share this feeling with the group. He wanted to be a part of the group, to be liked and accepted; but he also wanted to be his own person, to run with no gang, and to be accepted as he was.

After being a member of the gang for six months, Manuel had a long talk with his cousin, also a gang member. During the course of the evening, Manuel shared several of his thoughts and feelings about being in the gang. His cousin said, "Boy, if I had those feelings, I sure wouldn't be in a gang. It is right that you do what is important for you, to be your own man, and do what you need to do."

Several weeks later, Manuel took Permission from his cousin and left the gang to go his own way.

THE LOST BOSS

Common Myth of Bosses	*Myth-Breaker Permission*
As a boss, I have to be in control at all times. I am responsible for everything in my area.	I can be a boss and be real at the same time. I don't have to be responsible for everything.

PERMISSION FOR BOSSES TO BE REAL

If you, as a boss, decide to be real, you probably will feel a great burden being removed from your shoulders. Giving up the role of boss, with its accompanying responsibilities, will probably result in increased effectiveness. The Permission you give yourself will also provide effective modeling for your employees. Seeing you give up unnecessary reponsibilities will allow them to take on more fully their own responsibility, and will result in their increased self-respect.

Nadia was the president of a large cosmetics company. She was tense and anxious most of the time and developed an ulcer. She consulted a therapist, who supported her as she became aware of how and why she made herself physically ill. Nadia discovered that, as a boss, she thought she had to have complete control over and responsibility for everything and everybody. The therapist gave her Permission to give up total control, to let her realness emerge, and to flow more with the firm's problems. She took his Permission and began working in a more relaxed manner. Several months later her ulcer disappeared.

THE PERFECT TEACHER

<table>
<tr><td>Common Myth of Teachers</td><td>Myth-Breaker Permission</td></tr>
<tr><td>I, as an authority, must know everything and have all the answers, or my students will think I'm stupid.</td><td>Even as an authority, I don't have all the answers. I can say, "I don't know," when I really don't know.</td></tr>
</table>

PERMISSION FOR TEACHERS TO GIVE UP BEING PERFECT

In your process of deciding to be real, you will not only be giving yourself Permission, you will be modeling the same Permission for your students. They probably will be relieved to know that you are not perfect and that they don't have to be perfect either.

During her student-teaching experience, Sylvia felt a lot of anxiety about entering a classroom. One day a student asked Sylvia a question she could not answer. Sylvia froze, cleared her throat, and stammered. Finally, the teacher in charge answered the question for Sylvia. During recess, the supervising teacher asked Sylvia why she had behaved as she had. Sylvia explained that she didn't know the answer and didn't want the students to think that she was "dumb."

The supervisor, understanding Sylvia's fear, said, "The students don't expect you to know everything. It is fine for you to say you don't know the answer. You could tell them that you don't know but will find out later." Sylvia remembered her supervising teacher's Permission and found herself much more relaxed in the classroom.

COUPLE TROUBLE

<table>
<tr><td>Common Myth of Relationships</td><td>Myth-Breaker Permission</td></tr>
<tr><td>Because we are in a close relationship, we must be all things to each other and must totally satisfy each other's needs.</td><td>We can be in a close relationship and not have to be all things to each other. We do not have to totally satisfy each other's needs. We can reach out to others outside of our relationship without taking something away from each other.</td></tr>
</table>

PERMISSION TO REMAIN AN INDIVIDUAL IN A RELATIONSHIP

It may be difficult to relinquish the above myth, but once you are released from its bond, you will experience a tremendous sense of freedom. Shared efforts will be necessary for the two of you to break this pervasive myth. You may give Permission to each other and to yourselves as you work together. Actually, there is no way in which two people can meet all of each other's needs. So stop trying! Get on with being the two individuals and unique persons you really are.

Ike and Tina dated all through high school and college. Their only fighting occurred when Ike said he needed other friends and would even like to date someone else to see what other women were like. Tina felt very threatened because she thought she had to be everything to Ike and meet all his needs. She experienced a sense of failure when Ike talked about wanting to be with others. Eventually, Ike left the restrictive relationship.

Ike later met Marcia, a woman who thought that she and Ike could meet many of each other's needs and desires but who sensibly believed that some of their wants and needs could be met by others. Their relationship culminated in marriage, but the marriage did not change Ike and Marcia's thoughts about including others.

XVIII LOVE YOURSELF TODAY MORE THAN YOU DID YESTERDAY AND NOT AS MUCH AS YOU WILL TOMORROW

> HE THAT FALLS IN LOVE
> WITH HIMSELF WILL HAVE
> NO RIVALS.
>
> *POOR RICHARD'S ALMANACK*
> —BENJAMIN FRANKLIN

EPILOGUE

Congratulations for courageously reading through this book and examining the variety of ways you limit or have limited yourself from living freely. As you already know, through the process of understanding yourself, you may have experienced varying feelings of joy, anger, even panic. Therefore, you deserve credit for standing by yourself through the best and through the worst . . . even if you received this book, anonymously, wrapped in plain brown paper, with certain reactions underlined for your benefit.

It is fine for you to continue your journey of self-understanding instead of avoiding yourself. You are lovable, intelligent, capable, courageous, and uniquely valuable. You can be any way you choose to be, you can do everything, or you can do nothing. Your final redecisions—forgiving your parents, getting Permissions from others, giving yourself Permissions, rewriting your script, and keeping current with yourself—are ultimately up to you.

In this book, we have been like loving friends, gently nudging you out of your old nest (script patterns) and giving you Permission to go ahead and fly—to be as beautiful and free as you can be. And now we say: Continue to greet the highest in yourself, and may Permissions continue to be an important part of your life.

NOTES AND SOURCES

For complete publication information consult the Bibliography.

ACKNOWLEDGMENTS

1. The major published source on their work is a chapter written by Robert Goulding, "New Directions in Transactional Analysis: Creating an Environment for Redecision and Change," contained in *Progress in Group and Family Therapy*, by Sager and Kaplan. The Gouldings have a new work in progress on redecisions. Its title is *Redecision Therapy* and was published by Brunner-Mazel Publishers, New York.
2. Permission Theory is a comprehensive theory of human behavior that draws compatible elements from other less comprehensive but equally valid theories.

CHAPTER I.
PERMISSIONS: A BASIC TOOL FOR CHANGE

1. From *Rebirthing in the New Age*, by Leonard Orr and Sondra Ray.
2. From "Injunctions, Decisions and Redecisions," *Transactional Analysis Journal*, January 1976.
3. From *The Politics of Experience*, by R. D. Laing.
4. From *Family Circle*, March 27, 1978.

CHAPTER III.
PERMISSION PATTERNS

1. From *The Prophet*.
2. This inventory was developed by one of the coauthors, Barry K. Weinhold.

CHAPTER V.
TRACING THE TIES TO YOUR PAST

1. The basic work on the effects of unresolved symbiosis was done by Jacqui Schiff and the members of the Cathexis Institute in Oakland, California. Two major sources on this work are *All My Children*, by Jacqui and Moe Schiff, and *The Cathexis Reader*, by Jacqui Schiff, et al.
2. This chart was developed from information presented at the Rocky Mountain Regional Transactional Analysis Conference in Denver, Colorado, April 1976, by Ms. Dorothy Babcock and Dr. Terry Keepers. See *Raising Kids O.K.*, by Babcock and Keepers, for more complete information on normal development.
3. These concepts were derived from the terms "potency," "permissions," and "protection," first used by Eric Berne to describe the functions of an effective therapist. Besides objecting to the possible sexist connotations of "potency," the authors are using these terms to represent a broader class of natural therapeutic processes that extends beyond the therapist's office.

CHAPTER VI.
PARDON ME, YOUR SCRIPT IS SHOWING

1. The idea for this section came from the short essay "On Parenting" by Henry Close.
2. Torrey's essay appeared in the March 1977 issue of *Psychology Today*.
3. For more help on how to suffer see *How to Make Yourself Miserable* by Dan Greenberg. He does a fine parody on how people invest time and energy in being miserable.
4. The concept of figure-ground is central to Gestalt Therapy. The theory emphasizes that owing to early traumatic situations, people have difficulty coping effectively with similar situation where the figure-ground is not complete.

This figure is one that has been used in the classical research in gestalt psychology, where it was shown that even though both the vase and faces are visible, it is impossible to focus on both at the same time.

5. Bandler and Grinder, in their book *The Structure of Magic, Volume II,* indicate that people have favorite ways of representing their experiences to themselves and others. They believe that the words people use indicate whether their favorite system is visual ("I *see* what you mean"), auditory ("I *hear* what you are saying"), or kinesthetic ("I have a *feel* for where you are"). According to their theory, the best position is to be free to use all three systems interchangeably.

CHAPTER VII.
THE MEDIUM IS THE MESSAGE

1. A book by Bruno Bettelheim, *The Uses of Enchantment,* takes an in-depth look at the place of fairy tales in the lives of children. Bettelheim agrees that one advantage of fairy tales is their presentation of clear-cut characters for children to identify with.
2. From a news article in *Family Weekly,* May 8, 1977.
3. From "The Scary World of TV's Heavy Viewer," *Psychology Today,* April 1976.
4. Ibid.
5. Ibid.
6. From an Associated Press news article appearing in *The Gazette Telegraph,* Colorado Springs, Colorado, March 1977.
7. From the *National Analysis of Official Child Neglect and Abuse Reporting: An Executive Summary,* American Humane Society, Englewood, Colorado, 1978.
8. From *Understanding Child Neglect and Abuse,* American Humane Society, Englewood, Colorado, 1978.

CHAPTER VIII.
IT'S NOT TOO LATE TO CHANGE YOUR FATE

1. From *Future Shock,* by Alvin Toffler.
2. Ibid.
3. From *Statistical Abstract of the United States* for 1976.
4. From a reprint of a speech by the Simontons in

Journal of Transpersonal Psychology, 1976.
5. Adapted from information on banal scripts by Hogie Wycoff in Steiner's *Scripts People Live.*

CHAPTER IX.
DECISIONS, DECISIONS, DECISIONS

1. From an article by Maya Pines in *APA Monitor,* December 1975. A more complete report of Dr. Garmezy's work is available from the American Psychological Association, Washington, D.C.

CHAPTER XI.
FORGIVING YOUR PARENTS

1. Sheehy points out in *Passages* that most people resist as long as they can the realization that they are separate. The main way they do this is by blaming others for what has happened to them. She says, "But by giving up the illusion [that others are to blame], what is to be gained is no less than the full release of our freely authentic selves."

CHAPTER XII.
USING PERMISSIONS FROM OTHERS TO UNRAVEL YOUR MYSTERIES

1. The International Transactional Analysis Association publishes an annual membership list that includes over 10,000 regular and advanced members, listed by state. This can be useful if you are looking for a therapist in your state or city. Information on obtaining the directory can be received by writing ITAA, 1772 Vallejo Street, San Francisco, California 94123.

CHAPTER XIII.
GIVING YOURSELF PERMISSIONS TO UNRAVEL YOUR MYSTERIES

1. This term was used in an article by Bob Samples, which appeared in the *Association for*

Humanistic Psychology Newsletter, May 1977.

CHAPTER XIV.
WEAVING TOGETHER THE THREADS OF THE NEW YOU

1. State licensing laws, in the name of consumer protection, have restricted the practice of psychology to a select few Ph.D.-level psychologists and Masters in Social Work. This has functioned to restrict the supply of available therapists and to increase the cost of the service to the consumer.
2. Thanks to Betty Fuller, a workshop leader at Esalen Institute, for introducing us to this concept, which we assume was not original with her.

CHAPTER XV.
USING PERMISSIONS TO CHANGE YOUR LIFE DECISIONS

1. Development is continuous. Sheehy in *Passages* states, "The whole idea behind developmental change is that things can never be settled once and for all."
2. Sheehy again captures the limiting qualities of childhood script decisions. "From the childhood identifications with our parents we carry along the most primitive layer of imaginary protection. . . ." She adds, "It is this internalized protection that gives us a sense of insula-
tion and . . . shields us from coming face to face with our own absolute separateness." She concludes: "But it is an illusion" that ". . . does nothing actually to protect us from being separate."
3. Sheehy writes about recycling. "The catch is, inner issues pushed down in one period tend to swing up in the next one with an added wallop."
4. Robert and Mary Goulding have been primarily responsible for the basic work on redecisions and the redecision process. The most complete description of this work can be found in *Progress in Group and Family Therapy,* edited by Sager and Kaplan.

CHAPTER XVI.
USING PERMISSIONS TO STAY CURRENT WITH YOURSELF

1. From *The World of the Contemporary Counselors,* by Gilbert Wrenn.
2. Quote from Gail Sheehy, *Passages.*
3. Ibid.
4. Ibid.
5. An excellent reference on journal keeping is a book by Ira Progoff, *At a Journal Workshop: The Basic Test and Guide for Using the Intensive Journal.*
6. Adapted from a similar activity in *The Truth About Psychology,* by Leonard Orr.
7. Ibid.
8. Adapted from a similar activity in *Group Methods to Actualize Human Potential* by Herbert Otto.
9. Adapted from Progoff's *At a Journal Workshop.*

BIBLIOGRAPHY

Babcock, Dorothy E., and Keepers, Terry D. *Raising Kids O.K.* New York: Grove Press, Inc., 1976.

Bandler, Richard, and Grinder, John. *The Structure of Magic, Volume II.* Palo Alto, California: Science & Behavior Books, Inc., 1976.

Berne, Eric. *What Do You Say After You Say Hello?* New York: Grove Press, Inc., 1978.

Bernhard, Yetta. *Self-Care.* Millbrae, California: Celestial Arts Publishing Co., 1975.

Bettelheim, Bruno. *The Uses of Enchantment: The Meaning and Importance of Fairy Tales.* New York: Alfred A. Knopf, Inc., 1976.

Bolles, Richard Nelson. *What Color Is Your Parachute?* Berkeley: Ten-Speed Press, 1974.

Cameron, Duncan. "Paving the Road to Redecision," in *Transactional Analysis Journal,* Vol. 6 (1976).

Churchill, Winston S. *My Early Life: A Roving Commission.* New York: Chas. A. Scribner Inc., 1930.

Close, Henry. "On Parenting," in *Voices: The Art and Science of Psychotherapy,* Vol. 4 (1968).

Costello, R. Kennon. "Consolidating Injunctions," in *Transactional Analysis Journal,* Vol. 6 (1976).

Dostoyevsky, Feodor. *The Brothers Karamazov.* New York: Bantam Books, 1970.

Ellis, Albert. *How to Live With a "Neurotic."* (Rev. ed) New York: Crown Publishers, 1975.

———. *Humanistic Psychotherapy: The Rational-Emotive Approach.* New York: Julian Press and McGraw-Hill Paperbacks, 1974.

———, and Harper, Robert A. *A New Guide to Rational Living.* Englewood Cliffs, New Jersey: Prentice-Hall and Hollywood: Wilshire Books, 1975.

Festing, Jones H. (ed.). *Notebooks of Samuel Butler.* New York: R-West, 1978.

Garmezy, Norman. *Vulnerable and Invulnerable Children: Theory, Research and Invention.* Washington D.C.: American Psychological Association, 1977.

Gerbner, George, and Gross, Larry. "The Scary World of TV's Heavy Viewer," in *Psychology Today,* Vol. 9 (April 1976).

Gibran, Kahlil. *The Prophet.* New York: Alfred A. Knopf, Inc., 1923.

Gordon, Thomas. *Parent Effectiveness Training: The Tested New Way to Raise Responsible Children.* New York: Peter H. Wyden, Inc., 1970.

———. *Teacher Effectiveness Training.* New York: David McKay Co., Inc., 1975.

Goulding, Robert. "Decisions in Script Formation," in *Transactional Analysis Journal,* Vol. 2 (1972).

———. "New Directions in Transactional Analysis: Creating an Environment for Redecision and Change," in Sager and Kaplan, eds., *Progress in Group and Family Therapy,* q.v.

———, and Goulding, Mary. "Injunctions, Decisions and Redecisions," in *Transactional Analysis Journal,* Vol. 6 (1976).

Greenberg, Dan and Jacobs, Marcia. *How to Make Yourself Miserable.* New York: Random House, Inc., 1976.

Hammarskjöld, Dag. *Markings.* New York: Alfred A. Knopf, Inc., 1964.

Holder, Wayne M., and Schene, Patricia. *Understanding Child Neglect and Abuse.* Englewood, Colorado: American Humane Society, 1978.

Holt, John. *Escape From Childhood.* New York: Ballantine Books, 1976.

Hutschnecker, Arnold. *The Will to Live.* New York: Thomas Y. Crowell Co., 1953.

Kaufmann, Walter. *Without Guilt and Justice: From Decidlophobia to Autonomy.* New York: Peter H. Wyden, Inc., 1973.

Kinderlehrer, Jane. "Give Me the Marx Brothers. Give Me Vitamin C," in *Prevention,* Vol. 29 (1977).

Laing, R. D. *The Politics of Experience.* New York: Ballantine Books, 1978.

———. *The Facts of Life: An Essay in Feelings, Facts, and Fantasy.* New York: Pantheon Books, 1976.

Lawrence, Peter. *Peter's Quotations.* New York: Morrow, 1977.

Levin, Pam. *Becoming the Way We Are.* Berkeley, California: Transactional Publications, 1974.

Lewis, Howard R., and Streitfeld, Harold. *Growth Games.* New York: Bantam Books, Inc. 1972.

Maugham, W. Somerset. *A Writer's Notebook.* New York: Arno Press, 1977.

Montaigne, Michel de. *Essays.* New York: Gordon Press, 1975.

National Analysis of Official Child Neglect and Abuse Reporting: An Executive Summary. Englewood, Colorado: American Humane Society, 1978.

Nietzsche, Friedrich. *Ecce Homo.* New York: Gordon Press, 1974.

Orr, Leonard. *The Truth About Psychology.* San Francisco: Leonard Orr, 1976.

————,and Ray, Sondra. *Rebirthing in the New Age.* Millbrae, California: Celestial Arts, 1977.

Otto, Herbert. *Group Methods to Actualize Human Potential.* Beverly Hills: The Holistic Press, 1970.

Pines, Maya. "In Praise of the Invulnerables," in *The APA Monitor.* Washington, D.C.: American Psychological Association, December 1975.

Progoff, Ira. *At a Journal Workshop: The Basic Test and Guide for Using the Intensive Journal.* New York: Dialogue House Library, 1975.

Ray, Sondra. *I Deserve Love.* Millbrae, California: Celestial Arts, 1976.

Sager, Clifford, and Kaplan, Helen, eds. *Progress in Group and Family Therapy.* New York: Brunner-Mazel, 1972.

Samples, Bob. "Selfness . . . Seeds of a Transformation." *Association for Humanistic Psychology Newsletter.* San Francisco: Association for Humanistic Psychology, May 1977.

Schiff, Jacqui, and Day, Beth. *All My Children.* Moonachie, New Jersey: Pyramid Publications, 1977 (rev. ed.).

————, et al. *The Cathexis Reader.* Harper and Row, 1975.

Schopenhauer, Arthur. *The World as Will and Idea,* New York: AMS Press, 1976.

Selye, Hans. *Stress Without Distress.* Philadelphia: J. B. Lippincott Company, 1974.

Sheehy, Gail. *Passages.* New York: E. P. Dutton & Co., Inc., 1976.

Simonton, O. C., Matthews-Simonton, S., and Creighton, J. *Getting Well Again.* Los Angeles: J. P. Tarcher, Inc., 1978.

Simonton, Carl, and Simonton, Stephanie. "Belief Systems and Management of the Emotional Aspects of Malignancy," in *Journal of Transpersonal Psychology,* Vol. 6 (1976).

Smith, Manuel J. *When I Say No, I Feel Guilty.* New York: Bantam Books, Inc., 1975.

Statistical Abstract of the United States. Washington, D.C.: U.S. Department of Commerce, 1976.

Steiner, Claude. *Scripts People Live: Transactional Analysis of Life Scripts.* New York: Grove Press, Inc., 1974.

Thoreau, Henry D. *Walden.* New York: New American Library A Signet Classic, 1960.

Toffler, Alvin. *Future Shock.* New York: Bantam Books, Inc., 1970.

Torrey, E. Fuller. "A Fantasy Trial About a Real Issue," in *Psychology Today,* Vol. 10, March 1977.

Wood, Nancy. *Many Winters.* Garden City, New York: Doubleday and Co., Inc., 1974.

Wrenn, C. Gilbert. *The World of the Contemporary Counselor.* Boston: Houghton Mifflin, 1973.